George Orwell's
Nineteen Eighty-Four

Edited & with
an Introduction
by Harold Bloom

© 1998 by Chelsea House Publishers, a division of Main Line Book Co.

Introduction © 1996 by Harold Bloom

All rights reserved. No part of this publication may be reproduced or transmitted in any form or by any means without the written permission of the publisher.

Printed and bound in the United States of America.

First Printing
1 3 5 7 9 8 6 4 2

ISBN: 0-7910-4140-9

Chelsea House Publishers
1974 Sproul Road, Suite 400
P.O. Box 914
Broomall, PA 19008-0914

Contents

Editor's Note	4
Introduction	5
Biography of George Orwell	7
Thematic and Structural Analysis	9
List of Characters	25
Critical Views	
Fredric Warburg: The Novel as a Terrifying Work	27
Julian Symons: The Virtues and Flaws of the Novel	28
George Orwell: The Thrust of the Novel	29
Daniel Bell: The Scope of the Novel	30
Aldous Huxley: Is the Novel's Prediction Plausible?	32
Stephen Spender: Evil in the Novel	33
Irving Howe: Orwell and Totalitarianism	34
A.E. Dyson: The Culmination of Orwell's Career	36
George Woodcock: Orwell and Family Life	39
Raymond Williams: Orwell, Totalitarianism, and Capitalism	40
Gorman Beauchamp: Sexuality as Political Defiance	42
William Steinhoff: Orwell and James Burnham	44
Lillian Feder: Language and Selfhood in the Novel	46
Paul Ehrlich and Anne Ehrlich: Orwell and Population	49
W.F. Bolton: Orwell and Language	52
Lynette Hunter: The Ending of the Novel	54
Daphne Patai: Women in the Novel	57
Mark Crispin Miller: The Novel and Television	59
Mark Connelly: Winston Smith and History	61
Patrick Reilly: Moral Choice	63
Michael Shelden: Autobiographical Elements in the Novel	65
W.J. West: The Novel and Surveillance	67
Books by George Orwell	70
Works About George Orwell and *Nineteen Eighty-Four*	72
Index of Themes and Ideas	76

Editor's Note

My Introduction emphasizes both the aesthetic limitations and the continued political relevance of *Nineteen Eighty-Four*. Critical Views begin with the book's first publisher, Fredric Warburg, who conveys the terror of its vision and identifies the vision with Stalin's regime. Julian Symons finds the novel to be at once realistic and grotesque, while Orwell himself defends his moral purpose, a defense enhanced by the sociologist Daniel Bell, who states the narrative's relevance to America.

In a letter to Orwell, Aldous Huxley intimates that his own *Brave New World* is a likelier prophecy than Oceania is, after which Stephen Spender speculates on the religious origins of Big Brother. The critic Irving Howe commends Orwell's political insight, while A. E. Dyson evaluates *Nineteen Eighty-Four* as an ironic masterwork. George Woodcock aptly sees Orwell's horror at the destruction of familial loyalties, but Raymond Williams accuses the author of political confusions.

Whether Gorman Beauchamp's emphasis upon Orwell's exaltation of sexuality as a mode of political resistance, in the book, can be justified, is unclear to me; I am more persuaded by Lillian Feder's observations on the language of selfhood as a more reliable defense against Big Brother.

Paul and Anne Ehrlich fault Orwell for not having prophesied the world's population explosion, while W. F. Bolton praises him for his insights into the language of politics.

The book's ending, in which poor Winston is broken, is analyzed by Lynette Hunter, after which Daphne Patai criticizes Orwell from a Feminist perspective. More unsettling are Mark Crispin Miller's observations on the affinities between our passive relation to television and Winston's condition at the book's conclusion.

Our differences from Winston are urged by Mark Connelly and Patrick Reilly, while Michael Shelden shrewdly shows how much of the book is based upon Orwell's own life. In a final extract, W. J. West makes a very unsettling analogue between Orwell's prophecy and many features of thought-control in our current society.

Introduction

HAROLD BLOOM

Reading *Nineteen Eighty-Four* in 1995, and after, presents problems not altogether present from 1949, the book's date of publication, on through some thirty-five years later, its projected date of fulfillment. Orwell died in 1950 of tuberculosis when he was only forty-six. Whether in the year 2000 we will judge *Nineteen Eighty-Four* to have been an accurate prophecy is still uncertain. We have gone further in the technological developments that would make the novel's tyranny even more feasible. Politicians on television nightly instruct us in newspeak and doublethink, and the United Nations, in Bosnia and elsewhere, practices "peacekeeping" and creates "safe areas," whose burden might as well be "War Is Peace." Hollywood's spate of "dumb" films, of the *Forrest Gump* variety, do proclaim that "Ignorance Is Strength," and many of our African-American intellectuals rightly judge Speaker Gingrich to be telling them that "Freedom Is Slavery," particularly when he urges restoring to the poor their freedom to starve. Big Brother presumably is not *yet* watching us, and we have given up, for now, putting Saddam Hussein on-screen for the Two Minutes Hate. Even if we had a Ministry of Truth, it would now probably be underfunded in our zeal to abolish government, that enemy of the sacred profit motive which forms our authentic spirituality, the basis for the Christian Coalition.

In so gladsome a time, *Nineteen Eighty-Four* is not likely to lose relevance. It is, in fact, at best a good "bad book," inept as narrative, and worse than that as characterization. The book continues to have moral force as a political early warning and truly is what I once called it, the *Uncle Tom's Cabin* of our time. Actually, it is aesthetically inferior to Harriet Beecher Stowe's novel. Stowe knew better how to tell a story, and Uncle Tom is a more interesting martyr than Orwell's failed martyr, the drab Winston Smith. I would rather attend to little Eva than to poor Julia, and the insane sadist O'Brien is considerably less impressive than the wicked Simon Legree. Wyndham Lewis sensibly compared Orwell as a writer to H. G. Wells, but Wells was consistently more inventive and entertaining. All this is not said to beat up on *Nineteen Eighty-Four,* but to point out that we do not go on reading the book because Orwell possessed a large talent for prose fiction. He did not; he was a moral and political essayist who had the instincts of a pamphleteer. A great pamphleteer, like Jonathan Swift, is a master of irony and satire. Here again, Orwell plainly is deficient. His literalness defeats his wit, such as it is, and his only ironic gift is as a good parodist of political slogans.

And yet *Nineteen Eighty-Four* survives and will have life whenever we are threatened with totalitarian utopias, whether political, economic, social, or theocratic. "Political correctness," our now-passing rage of liberal conformity, is very much an Orwellian phenomenon, and our universities, wretched parodies of what they are supposed to be, are veritable monuments of newspeak and doublethink. It is very difficult to say whether our current Left or our dominant Right is a more Orwellian grab bag, and our public life is mostly a parade marching toward his Oceania. Preachers of the Third Wave, who so enthrall Speaker Gingrich, propose a technology founded purely upon information. Orwell remains superbly valuable because no one warns us better that such a foundation in fact must and will give us only an orgy of disinformation. As hypertext and virtual reality usurp us in the computer era, Orwell's nightmare will come ever closer. Without being a great writer, or even a good novelist, Orwell nevertheless had the courage and foresight to see and tell us where we were going. We are still going there, and *Nineteen Eighty-Four* holds on as an admonition telling us to turn back. ✤

Biography of George Orwell

George Orwell was the pseudonym of Eric Arthur Blair, who was born on June 25, 1903, in Motihari, Bengal, the son of a minor British official in India. When Orwell was two he returned to England with his mother and older sister. The family was able to save enough money to send their only son to St. Cyprian's, an expensive private school near Eastbourne. There Orwell won scholarships to Wellington and, in 1917, to Eton, where he spent four years. Although an excellent (albeit unhappy) student at St. Cyprian's, Orwell showed little interest in his studies at Eton. Instead of going on to university like most of his classmates, he became an officer in the Burmese Imperial Police.

Orwell's five years in Burma were dismal. In his first novel, *Burmese Days* (1934), he painted a highly critical portrait of the British community there. In 1927 he returned to England, penniless and without prospects. For several years he lived in London and then Paris, earning only enough money to feed himself. His experiences among the world of day laborers, itinerant hop pickers, and restaurant employees were chronicled in his first published book, *Down and Out in Paris and London* (1933).

Although his early ambition was to write "a neat shelf of realistic novels," Orwell's growing involvement in political debate impinged more and more on his literary career as the 1930s progressed. Following two minor novels (*A Clergyman's Daughter* [1935], and *Keep the Aspidistra Flying* [1936]), he was commissioned in 1936 to write a book-length report on the living conditions of miners in the north of England. This study was published by the Left Book Club as *The Road to Wigan Pier* (1937). The following year Orwell went to Spain to cover the civil war there and wound up as a captain in the military arm of a syndicalist party fighting against the Falangist insurgents. After many months at the front he was shot through the neck, sustaining a permanent injury to his vocal cords, and returned behind the lines just in time to find that his faction had been denounced by its Communist partners and was being systematically purged. With his wife of one year, Eileen O'Shaughnessy, he escaped across the border to France and returned to England, where he published *Homage to Catalonia* (1938), an account of his Spanish adventure.

In 1939 Orwell published a fourth novel, *Coming Up for Air,* and continued to write political commentary and reviews. Once World War II broke out he joined the Home Guard and began to work for the BBC in its Indian Division, producing presentations of political and literary commentary for broadcast in India. (These pieces were later published in 1985 as *The War Broadcasts* and *The War Commentaries.*) In 1943 he left that position after disputes with his superiors over the censorship of war news and took a position as literary editor of the *Tribune,* a left-wing weekly for which he also wrote a column for several years entitled "As I Please." During this time he also composed a brief satirical fable about Stalinism, which after many rejections was published in 1945 as *Animal Farm.* In the same year his wife died suddenly, leaving the chronically ill Orwell to raise their adopted infant son.

Increasingly hampered by pneumonia, Orwell spent his final years on the Outer Hebrides island of Jura, working on his last novel, *Nineteen Eighty-Four* (1949). This bitter and compelling dystopian fantasy of the ultimate totalitarian future was an immediate worldwide success, but Orwell failed to live long enough to reap its rewards. After entering a London hospital for treatment of his tuberculosis in late 1949, he married a young editorial assistant, Sonia Brownell, in a bedside ceremony. A month later, on January 21, 1950, he died following severe hemorrhaging in one lung.

In his short life George Orwell managed to leave several works that would inspire and define debate across the political spectrum for decades following. He is also regarded as among the finest essayists in modern English literature, and his *Collected Essays, Journalism and Letters* appeared in four volumes in 1968. ✣

Thematic and Structural Analysis

In *Nineteen Eighty-Four,* George Orwell's nightmarish tale of a dystopian future, the Party, which rules one of the world's three great political divisions, exerts near-total control over its citizens. **Part one** of the novel describes the predicament of a discontented member of the Outer Party (the wing of the Party with no real power). The novel's opening line begins routinely but ends on a discordant note: "It was a bright cold day in April, and the clocks were striking thirteen" (**chapter one**). The omniscient narrator proceeds to introduce the protagonist, Winston Smith, a thirty-nine-year-old Party member with a painful varicose ulcer on his ankle. Winston lives in a dilapidated apartment building in London, chief city of Airstrip One (formerly Great Britain), a province of Oceania. As he climbs the seven flights of stairs to his flat, he passes a huge poster on each floor depicting the Party's mythical and omnipresent leader, Big Brother. The caption reads, "BIG BROTHER IS WATCHING YOU," and the truth of that statement soon becomes evident. Inside his flat—and, we will discover, throughout the public and private spaces of Oceania—a telescreen commands a strategic view. This device, which cannot be turned off, is used for broadcasting news and music but also permits audio and visual surveillance any time of the day by the Thought Police, whose function is to ferret out and punish any deviation from the established orthodoxy.

Winston tries to remember what life was like during his childhood, before the Party took over, but can only recall a few contextless images. Curiosity about the past, both personal and societal, forms much of Winston's intellectual life and will loom large in his demise. He reflects on the regime's four ministries: the Ministry of Truth, in charge of all news and entertainment; the Ministry of Plenty, which controls the economy; the Ministry of Peace, which prosecutes wars; and, most frightening of all, the Ministry of Love, into whose huge, windowless headquarters criminals disappear.

By some fluke in design, a tiny alcove in Winston's flat is outside the direct view of the telescreen. He now retreats to this alcove with a pen and a blank book he has secretly purchased. He intends to start a diary, an action that—though technically not illegal, as all laws have been abolished—would probably be punished by death if discovered.

After writing the date, April 4th, 1984, he hesitates, realizing that he cannot be sure that it really is 1984. He is also not sure why he wants to keep a diary: If the future is like the present, no one will heed what he writes; if it is different, no one will understand his predicament. Nevertheless, he begins writing about the war movie he saw the previous night, which triggers the memory of an incident that occurred this morning—an incident that, he suddenly realizes, is his impetus for keeping the diary. It happened at the Ministry of Truth, where he works, after the Two Minutes Hate (a regular activity during which Party workers gather to watch telescreen images of Oceania's enemies—primarily Emmanuel Goldstein, a legendary traitor rumored to be the head of a group of conspirators known as the Brotherhood—and drive themselves into a "hideous ecstasy of fear and vindictiveness, a desire to kill, to torture, to smash faces in"). As the image of Big Brother appeared on-screen along with three slogans of the party—WAR IS PEACE, FREEDOM IS SLAVERY, and IGNORANCE IS STRENGTH—Winston's eyes had briefly met those of a man named O'Brien. At that moment, he discerned that O'Brien, a member of the elite Inner Party, which holds the reins of power, shared his hatred of the system and Big Brother—a discovery that had given him hope. Winston had also noticed a dark-haired young woman who, he knew, worked in the Fiction Department; she was especially emphatic in her denunciation of Goldstein. Imagining her to be a Party zealot—and resentful of the red sash proclaiming her membership in the Junior Anti-Sex League, a Party organization promoting total abstinence—he had fantasized about raping and murdering her.

As his recollections of the Two Minutes Hate fade, Winston sees that he has unconsciously been writing over and over again in his diary, "DOWN WITH BIG BROTHER." In a panic, he realizes that this is evidence of the crime he committed by merely thinking ill of the Party—"thoughtcrime," "the essential crime that contained all others in itself." He imagines his inevitable arrest and execution but writes, *"they'll shoot me in the back of the neck i don't care down with big brother."* Upon hearing a knock at the door, he starts violently.

Winston answers the door and discovers, to his relief, that it is his neighbor, Mrs. Parsons, whose kitchen sink is blocked (**chapter two**). After helping her, he returns to his flat and begins thinking of O'Brien again. He recalls that, about seven years ago, he had a dream in which he was walking through a dark room. A voice that he later identified as O'Brien's said to him, "We shall meet in the place where there is no darkness." Though he has never understood the meaning of those words, he knows somehow that they will come true. In *Nineteen Eighty-Four* dreams both connect the protagonist with his forgotten past and presage his terrible future.

That night, Winston dreams of his mother and baby sister— who disappeared, he believes, sometime during the 1950s (**chapter three**). He knows that somehow their deaths made it possible for him to continue living, but he is unsure how. He also dreams that he is in a peaceful landscape he may or may not have once seen, which he calls the Golden Country. The dark-haired woman from the Fiction Department approaches him and with a single graceful movement tears off her clothes, an action that seems to sweep away the authority of Big Brother and the Party. The dream is interrupted by a piercing whistle from the telescreen that wakes up Party members and calls them to morning calisthenics. As his body follows the on-screen exercise instructor, Winston's mind wanders to a childhood memory of an air raid, and he reflects that since that time war has been almost continuous. At present, Oceania is at war with Eurasia and allied with Eastasia. According to the Party, Oceania has always been at war with Eurasia and allied with Eastasia, but Winston knows this not to be true. He remembers that just four years ago Eastasia was the enemy. Were he a faithful member of the Party, Winston would overcome such cognitive dissonance through "doublethink," the mental process whereby unsanctioned or contradictory thoughts and memories are forgotten while the process of forgetting them is itself forgotten, so that one is "conscious of complete truthfulness while telling carefully constructed lies." As Winston begins to recall the one time in his life he had irrefutable proof that the Party had lied, the exercise instructor yells at him through the telescreen because he is not touching his toes.

The action moves to Winston's work in the Records Department of the Ministry of Truth (**chapter four**). His job involves altering (in the language of the Party, "rectifying") news items or articles that have been published but that no longer reflect the Party line. A newspaper account from the previous year, for example, detailed Big Brother's praise of a certain Comrade Withers, an Inner Party member who has since been purged. Enemies of the Party are rarely tried publicly but are simply "vaporized"—secretly executed with all traces of their existence, including references in print, destroyed. Thus in Winston's rewrite of the newspaper account, Big Brother praises a fictitious war hero.

In the workers' cafeteria, Winston is joined by Syme, a philologist from the Research Department engaged in compiling the definitive edition of the Newspeak dictionary (**chapter five**). Newspeak is the official language of the Party, and Syme explains that its ultimate goal is to "narrow the range of thought" by eliminating "unnecessary" words. "In the end," he says enthusiastically, "we shall make thoughtcrime literally impossible because there will be no words in which to express it." (In an **appendix** Orwell fleshes out this and other principles of Newspeak.) Soon they are joined by Winston's overweight and obtuse neighbor, Parsons, who is organizing their apartment building's activities for the approaching Hate Week and solicits a contribution. While the large cafeteria telescreen announces a fabulous increase in the production of consumer goods and an accompanying rise in the standard of living, Winston thinks about how dreary the physical texture of life really is and wonders if it has always been so. After the announcement, he notices that the dark-haired woman is looking at him and concludes that, if not actually a member of the Thought Police, she must at least be an amateur spy. He worries that his face may have betrayed his discontent.

In the next two chapters, diary entries spur unpleasant memories for Winston. He begins writing about a debasing encounter he had some years before with an old, toothless prostitute (**chapter six**). Soon he recalls his wife, Katharine, from whom he has long been separated (divorce not being permitted for Party members). Though she had "not a thought in her head that was not a slogan, and there was no imbecility . . . that she was not capable of swallowing if the Party handed it out to her," he could have lived with her were it not for her attitude toward sex. As soon as he touched her, she would wince and stiffen, submitting only because it was her "duty to the Party" to produce children. From early childhood Party members are conditioned to remove desire and pleasure from sex, and, as Winston observes, the "sexual act, successfully performed, [is] rebellion."

In another diary entry, Winston writes that if there is any hope for the future, it lies with the proles, the masses of laborers who make up some eighty-five percent of Oceania's population (**chapter seven**). In general, the Party interferes little in the lives of the proles: Few of them have telescreens in their homes and no attempt is made to indoctrinate them, though the Thought Police eliminate any who show signs of becoming dangerous. All that is required is that they continue to work and breed and that they possess "a primitive patriotism that could be appealed to whenever it [is] necessary to make them accept longer working hours or shorter rations." Although the Party claims to have freed them from capitalist slavery, "true to the principles of doublethink" it simultaneously holds that the proles are "natural inferiors who must be kept in subjection, like animals."

Winston begins copying a passage from a children's history book that describes how horrible life was under capitalism, before the Revolution thrust the Party into power. He realizes that there is no way to tell how much of it, if any, is true, because the Party saw to it that the "past was erased, the erasure was forgotten, the lie became truth." He recalls again the one time in his life that he had incontrovertible evidence of a deliberate falsification: a fragment of an old photograph that showed three since-executed Party members in New York at the time they had confessed to being in Siberia giving military secrets to the Eurasian general staff. Though the threat of physical pain frightens him, what Winston finds most intolerable about the Party is its intellectual tyranny—to survive, its members must deny the validity of their own experiences and memories. Perhaps, Winston briefly wonders, he is insane, for no one else seems to have a problem doing this.

The first part of the novel concludes with Winston wandering through a prole neighborhood (**chapter eight**). Hoping to find someone who can tell him what life was like before the Revolution, he follows an old man into a pub and buys him beer. Unfortunately, the man can focus only on trivial details— for example, that beer was cheaper—and Winston gives up. As he walks the streets, he recognizes the junk shop where he purchased his diary. The soft-spoken elderly proprietor, Mr. Charrington, sells him a glass paperweight in which is embedded a piece of coral, to which Winston is attracted not so much because it is beautiful, but because it conjures up a different, bygone era. After chatting for a while, Charrington shows Winston an unused room upstairs where, he says, he and his wife lived before her death. The room contains, among other things, a large bed and a picture of an old church. And, Winston cannot help noticing, there is no telescreen. When he leaves the junk shop, the dark-haired woman passes him on the pavement, looking directly into his eyes. Certain now that she has been spying on him—and that she has enough evidence to turn him in—he briefly entertains the possibility of following and killing her. But he is so paralyzed by fear that he cannot. When he returns home, his thoughts are again filled with images of his certain arrest, torture, and confession.

Part two of *Nineteen Eighty-Four* details Winston's clandestine relationship with the dark-haired woman, whose name, he will learn, is Julia. Four days after the encounter outside the junk shop, Winston is walking down a corridor in the Ministry of Truth when he notices her approaching from the other direction (**chapter one**). Her arm is in a sling, and she stumbles and falls onto the injured arm, crying out in pain. Instinctively Winston helps her up, and she furtively slips a small paper into his hands. Back at his desk, he reads the message: *"I love you."*

Exchanging even the few words necessary to arrange a meeting without arousing suspicion proves difficult. But eventually, after an agonizing week, Winston finds her at a table by herself in the cafeteria and sits nearby. Speaking in low tones and without looking at each other, they agree to meet that night in a public square—where, in the midst of a crowd and again without making eye contact, she gives Winston instructions for meeting her that weekend.

The place she has chosen for their rendezvous is outside the city, down a footpath and in a stand of trees (**chapter two**). It resembles the Golden Country, the idyllic landscape Winston has seen in his dreams. When Julia asks him what he thought of her before she slipped him the note, Winston confesses, to her delight, that he wanted to murder her. She reveals that she is "good at games": She always looks cheerful and takes a leading role in Party activities; she takes care to "yell with the crowd." Despite her membership in the Junior Anti-Sex League, she has had numerous love affairs. What, Winston wonders, has attracted her to him? "It was something in your face," she responds. "As soon as I saw you I knew you were against [the Party]." They make love, which Winston regards as a political act, "a blow struck against the Party."

In the succeeding weeks, though they meet frequently in the streets, they manage to have sex only once, in the belfry of a ruined church (**chapter three**). Julia, Winston learns, is just twenty-six and has no memories of the time before the Revolution. So while she loathes the Party, she accepts its existence as "unalterable." Unlike Winston, she has no interest in the intellectual horrors of Party doctrine. For her, life is quite simple: "You wanted a good time; . . . the Party . . . wanted to stop you having it; you broke the rules as best you could."

Though he knows it is dangerous, Winston decides to rent the room above Charrington's junk shop for his assignations with Julia (**chapter four**). The old proprietor seems both discreet and grateful for the extra money. In their secret room the two lovers luxuriate in simple pleasures the Party long ago banished from everyday life: real coffee, tea, and sugar, which Julia has obtained on the black market; makeup and perfume, which Party women cannot wear; and, most important, the freedom to make love when they choose and talk about what they choose. But the appearance of a rat from a hole in the wainscoting shatters the pleasure of their first meeting in the room. Winston, pale and faint, admits that he is terrified of rats.

Winston's friend Syme vanishes one day, and Winston soon realizes that he has been vaporized (**chapter five**). Though he and Julia know that the same end awaits them, Winston no longer finds life intolerable. The few hours of pleasure and freedom he and Julia manage to steal—indeed, the mere knowledge that the secret room exists—sustain him through the bleakness of his situation. Sometimes he and Julia talk vaguely of active rebellion against the Party, and he shares his belief that O'Brien can be trusted.

At the Ministry of Truth, O'Brien approaches Winston in a corridor and mentions that he enjoyed one of Winston's recent articles on Newspeak (**chapter six**). He says he has an advance copy of the tenth edition of the Newspeak dictionary and writes down his home address in case Winston would like to examine it. Winston believes this is a pretext for a personal meeting during which O'Brien could direct him into an anti-Party conspiracy.

In the secret room, Winston wakes up from an unsettling dream about his mother and sister (**chapter seven**). The dream triggers memories of a time during his childhood when he was between ten and twelve years old. A civil war was being fought or had recently ended, Winston's father had disappeared, and his mother seemed resigned to some terrible but never-enunciated impending event. One day, after Winston had snatched the family's entire chocolate ration and run for the door, he turned to see his mother hugging his sick sister, who was two or three years old. The gesture somehow conveyed that the girl was dying. Winston left, and when he returned several hours later, his mother and sister were gone, and he never saw them again.

The significance of the story, Winston tries to explain to Julia, lies in the hug: While it did not change anything, did not produce more chocolate or prevent their deaths, it was a human gesture. It expressed a kind of personal love and loyalty that the Party had convinced its members was of no account. Only among the proles do such feelings persist, for they are "not loyal to a party or a country or an idea" but to one another. "The proles are human beings," Winston observes. "We are not human." Julia and he then vow that when they are caught, they will remain loyal to each other. Undoubtedly they will confess, but that, Winston observes, "is not betrayal. What you say or do doesn't matter; only feelings matter. If they could make me stop loving you—that would be the real betrayal."

Winston and Julia go to O'Brien's flat (**chapter eight**). Escorted by his servant, they enter a richly furnished room where O'Brien is working. He turns off the telescreen—a privilege, he reveals, of the Inner Party. After some hesitation, Winston announces the reason for their visit: He and Julia believe O'Brien is involved in a secret conspiracy to overthrow the government, and they want to join. O'Brien instructs his servant to bring some wine—which Winston and Julia have never tasted—and proposes a toast to Emmanuel Goldstein, the leader, he says, of the conspiracy, which is indeed called the Brotherhood. O'Brien asks whether, if ordered to do so, the two are prepared to murder, commit acts of sabotage that might cause the deaths of innocent people, blackmail, corrupt children, spread venereal disease, and more. Winston and Julia say they are prepared to do anything—except to separate.

O'Brien asks Julia to leave first, to avoid attracting attention. Before Winston leaves, he arranges to get him a copy of Emmanuel Goldstein's book, which details what the Brotherhood is fighting for. O'Brien says hesitatingly that he and Winston will meet again. "In the place where there is no darkness?" Winston asks. O'Brien nods, seeming to understand the allusion.

Hate Week, the extended vilification of Oceania's enemy, Eurasia, takes an unexpected turn (**chapter nine**). On the sixth day, an Inner Party orator is delivering a speech condemning Eurasian atrocities when he is handed a piece of paper. Midsentence, with no pause or break in syntax, no change in his voice or manner, he substitutes Eastasia for Eurasia, and the crowd, realizing that Oceania is not at war with Eurasia, begins tearing down the incorrect posters and banners. Winston and the other workers at the Ministry of Truth spend a week of eighteen-hour days feverishly "rectifying" all the "obsolete" newspapers, books, pamphlets, films, sound tracks, and photographs. Only after it is "impossible for any human being to prove by documentary evidence that the war with Eurasia had ever happened" are the workers given time off.

Winston retreats to the secret room and begins reading Goldstein's book—*the book,* as it is referred to. Although it contains little that Winston does not already know, *the book* serves as an important plot device in *Nineteen Eighty-Four.* By reproducing the passages Winston reads, Orwell is able to provide a historical and political overview for his readers. We learn, for example, how the three superstates (Oceania, Eurasia, and Eastasia) came into being and what their boundaries are. We learn that their political systems are essentially the same; that their incessant warfare, though savage, is relatively limited in scope; and that no side can ever hope to conquer another, not even in alliance with the third. The principal motive of the warfare is to preserve the privileged position of the ruling oligarchies—in Oceania, the Inner Party—by disposing of surplus goods without raising the general standard of living (which would inevitably lead to greater education for the masses and, ultimately, dissatisfaction).

When Julia joins him in the secret room, Winston tells her that she must read *the book,* but she asks him to read it aloud. The chapter he begins details the principles of Ingsoc (Newspeak for "English Socialism," the political theory of the Party) and the techniques by which the Party perpetuates its position. Ingsoc denies that the past has any objective existence apart from the documentary record and people's memories. Because the Party controls the documentary record—and, to a great extent, people's memories—it controls the past. The past has to be altered for two reasons: to prevent people from being able to compare their present life with a past that might seem better, and to preserve the illusion of the Party's infallibility. But that illusion requires Party members' cooperation through the practice of doublethink, by which all contradictions can be reconciled in a kind of controlled insanity.

Winston notices that Julia has fallen asleep and shuts the book. He reflects that he understands how the Party operates but not why: What was the original motive behind its seizure of power? Though *the book* has not answered this question, it has confirmed for Winston that he is sane. What is true remains true even if only one person acknowledges it. "Sanity is not statistical," he murmurs before drifting off to sleep.

Winston and Julia awake to the sound of a prole woman's singing in the courtyard below (**chapter ten**). Though they toil from birth to death, the proles still manage to sing, Winston reflects. To them belongs the future, for one day they would become "a race of conscious beings."

"We are the dead," Winston says, which Julia dutifully repeats. "You are the dead," a voice from behind the picture on the wall says. In horror, Winston and Julia see the picture fall to the floor to reveal a telescreen. The voice orders them to stand back to back with their hands behind their heads. Soon a squad of black-uniformed men brandishing truncheons crashes into the room. One of them punches Julia in the stomach, and, as she gasps for breath, they drag her away. Winston wonders what they have done to Charrington, but when Charrington enters the room looking not like the kindly old proprietor but like a cold man of about thirty-five and gives orders to the guards, Winston realizes that he is a member of the Thought Police.

Part three describes Winston's interrogation and torture in the Ministry of Love. Initially he is taken to an ordinary prison, where he waits in a filthy holding cell with other criminals, including proles (**chapter one**). Then he is transferred by windowless van to a high-ceilinged, brightly lit cell somewhere in the Ministry of Love. He recognizes this as the place where there is no darkness: The building has no windows, and the lights are never turned off.

Other prisoners are led into the cell, including Ampleforth, a colleague of Winston's from the Ministry of Truth, and Winston's neighbor Parsons, who has been denounced for thoughtcrime by his young daughter. Most of the prisoners are at some point removed from the cell and taken to a "Room 101," which, judging by the hysterical reaction of an emaciated prisoner who seems to be acquainted with it, must be a horrible place.

A long time passes, and Winston, now alone in the cell, thinks that he would double his own pain if it would spare Julia, though he wonders whether it is possible to wish for an increase in pain when one is actually suffering. He hears the approach of footsteps. The door opens and O'Brien enters. "They've got you too!" Winston cries. But O'Brien steps aside to reveal the presence of a guard, saying, "You knew this, Winston. . . . You did know it—you have always known it," and Winston realizes that in some way he *has* always known that O'Brien is loyal to the Party. The guard smashes his elbow with a truncheon, producing excruciating pain. As he writhes on the floor Winston understands that it is impossible to wish for an increase in pain for any reason, that in "the face of pain there are no heroes."

Winston finds himself strapped to a bed with a bright light shining on his face and O'Brien standing over him (**chapter two**). He recalls the events that have occurred between the initial blow to his elbow and the present. After a period of routine savage beatings by guards, his interrogation was taken over by Party intellectuals, who, in sessions lasting for hours, relentlessly badgered and humiliated him, catching him in all kinds of supposed contradictions and lies. In the end he had confessed to a host of fictitious crimes, including murdering his wife, spying for Eastasia, assassinating prominent Party members, and being an associate of Emmanuel Goldstein.

Throughout his ordeal Winston had sensed that O'Brien was directing everything, although up to this point he had not actually seen him. Now O'Brien is the sole interrogator. He turns a dial, and the machine to which Winston is attached delivers a painful electric current. Whenever Winston gives him an unsatisfactory answer, he declares, he will turn the dial.

The questioning centers on Winston's insistence that a real past exists, independent of the Party's version. But O'Brien counters that the past exists only in records and in human memory, and because the Party controls both, it controls the past. Winston says that the Party has not controlled *his* memory. "On the contrary," O'Brien replies, "*you* have not controlled it. That is what has brought you here."

O'Brien goes on to say that reality is not objective and external; it exists only in the human mind. "Not in the individual mind, which can make mistakes, and in any case soon perishes; only in the mind of the Party, which is collective and immortal. Whatever the Party holds to be truth *is* truth," O'Brien says. He reminds Winston of a statement that he had written in his diary: "Freedom is the freedom to say that two plus two make four." He holds up four fingers and asks how many it would be if the Party said it was five. When Winston says four, he turns the dial and Winston receives the electric current. O'Brien repeats the question several times, but Winston continues to give the same answer, so he keeps increasing the current. Eventually, Winston is in so much pain that he perceives a "mysterious identity between five and four" but cannot say how many fingers O'Brien is holding up.

O'Brien interrupts the torture to explain that Winston has been brought to the Ministry of Love not to be punished but to be cured, to be made sane. "We do not merely destroy our enemies; we change them," he declares. Before he is annihilated Winston will truly have been converted.

The interrogation resumes with what appears to be an electroshock treatment, which produces "a large patch of emptiness" inside Winston's brain. In his disorientation he sees, for a fleeting moment, five fingers when O'Brien is actually holding up four. Satisfied with the progress, and declaring that he enjoys talking to Winston—whose mind, he says, resembles his own except for its insanity—O'Brien closes the session by allowing Winston to ask him a few questions. When asked about what has happened to Julia, he says that she readily betrayed Winston. When asked about Room 101, he replies, "You know what is in Room 101, Winston. Everyone knows. . . ."

After an indeterminate number of sessions that may have extended over several weeks, O'Brien explains that there are three stages to Winston's "reintegration"—learning, understanding, and acceptance—and that it is time to embark upon the second. Winston already knows *how* the Party maintains itself in power; O'Brien proceeds to tell him *why:*

> The Party seeks power entirely for its own sake. We are not interested in the good of others; we are interested solely in power. . . . We are different from all the oligarchies of the past. . . . They pretended, perhaps they even believed, that they had seized power unwillingly and for a limited time, and that just around the corner there lay a paradise where human beings would be free and equal. . . . We know that no one ever seizes power with the intention of relinquishing it. Power is not a means; it is an end.

O'Brien goes on to say that in the future there will be even more suffering, more treachery, more fear. Winston declares that a society founded on cruelty cannot endure, that the "spirit of Man" will ultimately prevail. O'Brien replies, "If you are a man, Winston, then you are the last man. Your kind is extinct; we are the inheritors." He asks whether Winston considers himself morally superior, and Winston says that he does. O'Brien then plays a tape recorded in his flat when Winston promised to commit all kinds of cruel acts if ordered by the Brotherhood. He then tells Winston to get up, take off his clothes, and look at himself in a full-length mirror on the other side of the room. The image Winston sees—of a bowed, ugly, skeletonlike "creature"—frightens and repulses him, and he collapses onto a stool and weeps. "We have beaten you, Winston," O'Brien declares. "You have seen what your body is like. Your mind is in the same state. . . . Can you think of a single degradation that has not happened to you?" Clinging to a last shred of humanity, Winston responds, "I have not betrayed Julia."

Weeks or months elapse, and, with his torture over, Winston's body has begun to heal (**chapter four**). He has capitulated and now sets about the task of reeducating himself. He concedes that sanity is statistical and, with a pencil provided to him, writes "FREEDOM IS SLAVERY" and "TWO AND TWO

MAKE FIVE." But one day, in the midst of a blissful reverie in which he sees himself waiting for the bullet that will end his life, he thinks of the Golden Country and says aloud, "Julia! Julia! Julia, my love! Julia!" Soon O'Brien comes to his cell and says, "You have had thoughts of deceiving me." Intellectually, he claims, Winston has very little wrong with him, but emotionally he has failed to make progress. He asks what Winston feels about Big Brother, and Winston responds that he hates him. Saying that Winston must love Big Brother, O'Brien orders him taken to Room 101.

Room 101, Winston discovers, contains each person's most elemental fear (**chapter five**). For him—as the Thought Police found out by monitoring Charrington's room—that is rats. O'Brien has a dual-compartment cage containing two large, hungry rats. The cage will be fitted to Winston's head, the gate separating the compartments will be opened, and the rats will eat out Winston's eyeballs or burrow through his cheeks and devour his tongue. As O'Brien moves the cage toward his face Winston screams, "Do it to Julia! . . . Tear her face off, strip her to the bones. Not me! Julia!" O'Brien removes the cage, for he has gotten what he wanted—Winston has betrayed Julia, breaking all bonds of love and loyalty.

The final scene takes place in the Chestnut Cafe—where, since his release, Winston has come to spend his afternoons drinking gin and perusing the newspaper (**chapter six**). This afternoon he is worried about developments on the African front and eagerly awaits news from the telescreen. He recalls the only time he has seen Julia since their arrest, a chance encounter in the park that inspired no feelings in him but that Julia seemed to find distasteful. They had both admitted to betraying the other. "Sometimes," Julia had said, "they threaten you with something . . . you can't even think about. And then you say, 'Don't do it to me, . . . do it to so-and-so' "—after which, she concludes, "you don't feel the same toward the other person any longer."

When the telescreen announces a glorious victory for Oceania on the African front, Winston is delirious with joy. Blissfully, he imagines himself back at the Ministry of Love, with all his past transgressions forgiven, as the bullet enters his brain. The novel's final line—"He loved Big Brother"—reveals that the Party's triumph over Winston is complete. ❖

—*Elizabeth Beaudin*
Yale University

List of Characters

Winston Smith is a discontented thirty-nine-year-old Party member employed in the Records Department of the Ministry of Truth, where his duties include revising previously published newspaper articles so that they fit the Party's current (but constantly changing) version of history. Although he finds the physical texture of life oppressive, what Winston most abhors is the intellectual dishonesty the Party demands. Accepting the Party requires denying rationality and common sense, along with a willful effort to suppress one's memories. In addition, the Party has destroyed personal love and loyalty and has thus, in Winston's view, taken away its members' humanity. His love affair with Julia is not only a dangerous rebellion against the Party but also an affirmation of human emotions. However, in the face of relentless torture, Winston eventually betrays Julia and completely accepts and internalizes Party doctrine, signalling the Party's ultimate triumph over the individual.

Julia is a twenty-six-year-old Party member who works in the Fiction Department of the Ministry of Truth. A member of the Junior Anti-Sex League and other Party organizations, she carefully cultivates the appearance of being a Party zealot to conceal her transgressions, including her sexual liaisons. She chooses Winston for a love affair because she senses in him a shared hatred of the Party. However, Julia's rebellion, unlike Winston's, stems not from revulsion with the Party's doctrine but from resentment that it stands in the way of a good time. Because of her youth, she has no recollections of life before the Party took power, and she accepts its existence as unchangeable.

O'Brien is an urbane official of the Inner Party—the actual rulers of Oceania—whom Winston mistakenly believes shares his dissatisfaction with the system. Knowing—from monitored conversations Winston and Julia had in their secret room—that Winston trusts him, O'Brien entices the lovers into expressing their desire to join an anti-Party conspiracy. After their arrest, he directs Winston's interrogation and torture, during which he demonstrates a keen and supple intellect as well as a ruthlessness in the service of the Party, to which he is completely dedicated.

Big Brother is the mythical leader of the Party whose handsome face adorns countless posters captioned "BIG BROTHER IS WATCHING YOU" and to whom all good things are attributed. Whether or not he is still alive—or ever existed—is irrelevant: It is easier to love an individual than an organization, and the Party uses Big Brother as a focus for its members' loyalty.

Emmanuel Goldstein—who, like Big Brother, may or may not exist—is a legendary traitor to the Party and the reputed leader of an anti-Party conspiracy called the Brotherhood. The Party uses him to focus its members' fear and hatred.

Mr. Charrington appears to be the kindly old proprietor of a prole junk shop. Winston decides to rent an unused room above his store, where he and Julia conduct their love affair. This turns out to be a costly mistake, for Charrington is actually a member of the Thought Police and monitors the lovers' activities and conversations through a hidden telescreen.

Syme, a colleague of Winston's from the Ministry of Truth, is a philologist who works on the new edition of the Newspeak dictionary. An enthusiastic member of the Party, he is nevertheless vaporized, presumably because he understands too well the ultimate purpose of Newspeak—to narrow the range of thought so that dissent is impossible to express.

Parsons, Smith's obtuse, irritating neighbor, reflexively accepts the Party's teachings. Nevertheless, his daughter, a member of the children's organization called the Spies, denounces him to the authorities when she hears him say "Down with Big Brother" in his sleep. ✤

Critical Views

FREDRIC WARBURG ON *NINETEEN EIGHTY-FOUR* AS A TERRIFYING WORK

[Fredric Warburg (1898–1981) was the founder of the publishing firm of Secker & Warburg, which published Orwell's *Nineteen Eighty-Four.* He is the author of *An Occupation for Gentlemen* (1959) and *All Authors Are Equal* (1973), a memoir of his years in publishing from which the following extract is taken. Here, Warburg reproduces his original publisher's report on Orwell's novel, in which he testifies to its terrifying power but notes that Orwell has supplied no explanation as to how society has lost its humanity.]

This is amongst the most terrifying books I have ever read. The savagery of Swift has passed to a successor who looks upon life and finds it becoming ever more intolerable. Orwell must acknowledge a debt to Jack London's *Iron Heel,* but in verisimilitude and horror he surpasses this not inconsiderable author. Orwell has no hope, or at least he allows his reader no tiny flickering candlelight of hope. Here is a study in pessimism unrelieved, except perhaps by the thought that, if a man can conceive *1984,* he can also will to avoid it. It is a fact that, so far as I can see, there is only one weak link in Orwell's construction; *he nowhere indicates the way in which man, English man, becomes bereft of his humanity.*

1984 is *Animal Farm* writ large and in purely anthropomorphic terms. One hopes (against hope?) that its successor will supply the other side of the picture. For what is *1984* but a picture of man unmanned, of humanity without a heart, of a people without tolerance or civilization, of a government whose *sole* object is the maintenance of its absolute totalitarian power by every contrivance of cruelty. Here is the Soviet Union to the nth degree, a Stalin who never dies, a secret police with every device of modern technology.
　　—Fredric Warburg, [Publishers report] (1948), *All Authors Are Equal* (London: Hutchinson, 1973), pp. 103–4

Julian Symons on the Virtues and Flaws of *Nineteen Eighty-Four*

[Julian Symons (1912–1994) was a prolific British critic and novelist. Among his critical works are *Mortal Consequences* (1972), a study of the detective story, *Critical Observations* (1981), and *Makers of the New: The Revolution in Literature 1912–1939* (1987). He also wrote many detective novels. In this review of *Nineteen Eighty-Four,* Symons praises the novel for its realism but finds the torture scenes toward the end more comical than horrifying.]

The picture of society in *Nineteen Eighty-Four* has an awful plausibility which is not present in other modern projections of our future. In some ways life does not differ very much from the life we live to-day. The pannikin of pinkish-grey stew, the hunk of bread and cube of cheese, the mug of milkless Victory coffee with its accompanying saccharine tablet—that is the kind of meal we very well remember; and the pleasures of recognition are roused, too, by the description of Victory gin (reserved for the privileged—the 'proles' drink beer), which has 'a sickly oily smell, as of Chinese rice-spirit' and gives to those who drink it 'the sensation of being hit on the back of the head with a rubber club.' We can generally view projections of the future with detachment because they seem to refer to people altogether unlike ourselves. By creating a world in which the 'proles' still have their sentimental songs and their beer, and the privileged consume their Victory gin, Mr Orwell involves us most skilfully and uncomfortably in his story, and obtains more readily our belief in the fantasy of thought-domination that occupies the foreground of his book. ⟨. . .⟩

Mr Orwell's book is less an example of any kind of Utopia than an argument, carried on at a very high intellectual level, about power and corruption. And here again we are offered the doubtful pleasure of recognition. Goldstein resembles Trotsky in appearance, and even uses Trotsky's phrase, 'the revolution betrayed'; and the censorship of Oceania does not greatly exceed that which has been practised in the Soviet Union, by the suppression of Trotsky's works and the creation of 'Trotskyism' as an evil principle. 'Doublethink,' also, has been a familiar feature of political and social life in more than one country for a quarter of a century.

The sobriety and subtlety of Mr Orwell's argument, however, is marred by a schoolboyish sensationalism of approach. Considered as a story, *Nineteen Eighty-Four* has other faults (some thirty pages are occupied by extracts from Goldstein's book, *The Theory and Practice of Oligarchical Collectivism*): but none so damaging as the inveterate schoolboyishness. The melodramatic idea of the Brotherhood is one example of it; the use of a nursery rhyme to symbolize the unattainable and desirable past is another; but the most serious of these errors in taste is the nature of the torture which breaks the last fragments of Winston's resistance. He is taken, as many others have been taken before him, to 'Room 101.' In Room 101, O'Brien tells him, is 'the worst thing in the world.' The worst thing in the world varies in every case; but for Winston, we learn, it is rats. The rats are brought into the room in a wire cage, and under threat of attack by them Winston abandons the love for Julia which is his last link with ordinary humanity. This kind of crudity (we may say with Lord Jeffrey) will never do; however great the pains expended upon it, the idea of Room 101 and the rats will always remain comic rather than horrific.

But the last word about this book must be one of thanks, rather than of criticism: thanks for a writer who deals with the problems of the world rather than the ingrowing pains of individuals, and who is able to speak seriously and with originality of the nature of reality and the terrors of power.
—Julian Symons, "Power and Corruption," *Times Literary Supplement,* 10 June 1949, p. 380

GEORGE ORWELL ON THE THRUST OF HIS NOVEL

[Upon publication of *Nineteen Eighty-Four,* George Orwell was quickly attacked by many leftists for what they felt was a betrayal of their cause. In the following letter, published in several magazines at the time, Orwell stresses that his novel is not an attack on socialism but a warning of the dangers of totalitarianism.]

My recent novel is NOT intended as an attack on Socialism or on the British Labour Party (of which I am a supporter) but as a show-up of the perversions to which a centralised economy is liable and which have already been partly realised in Communism and Fascism. I do not believe that the kind of society I describe necessarily *will* arrive, but I believe (allowing of course for the fact that the book is a satire) that something resembling it *could* arrive. I believe also that totalitarian ideas have taken root in the minds of intellectuals everywhere, and I have tried to draw these ideas out to their logical consequences. The scene of the book is laid in Britain in order to emphasise that the English-speaking races are not innately better than anyone else and that totalitarianism, *if not fought against,* could triumph anywhere.

—George Orwell, Letter to Francis A. Henson (16 June 1949), *Collected Essays, Journalism and Letters of George Orwell,* ed. Sonia Orwell and Ian Angus (New York: Harcourt Brace Jovanovich, 1968), Vol. 4, p. 502

DANIEL BELL ON THE SCOPE OF *NINETEEN EIGHTY-FOUR*

[Daniel Bell (b. 1919) is a distinguished American political and social critic and the author of such works as *The End of Ideology* (1962), *The Coming of Post-Industrial Society* (1973), and *The Cultural Contradictions of Capitalism* (1976). He is Henry Ford II Professor of Social Sciences at Harvard University. In this review of *Nineteen Eighty-Four,* Bell notes that its scope extends far beyond a satire of Soviet totalitarianism, and could just as well be directed toward disturbing trends in England and America.]

Nineteen Eighty-Four pictures life thirty years hence under *Ingsoc* (English Socialism), a unit of Oceania, one of three super-states in a permanent war for world hegemony. Ingsoc life is dingy, but if drabness were the only constituent element of Orwell's museum of horror, the novel and even Ingsoc life would be bearable. What makes it a shuddering, sickening, gripping spectacle is the remorseless piling on of detail upon detail, like a fingernail drawn ceaselessly across a blackboard, of a human society stripped of the last shreds of community, where even the sexual act is a cold, distasteful, jerky moment of copulation, performed because artificial methods are not yet sufficiently perfect to reproduce the species, and where fear and anxiety are the daily staple of life—not as in the concentration camps a dull and inured fear, but under the corrosive stimuli of hate, a high-tension, twitching exhaustion from which dreams and even sleep offer no escape. ⟨. . .⟩

Is this our world-to-be? Is this Socialism? Many will protest that Orwell has written an effective picture of totalitarianism, but not *democratic* Socialism. But other than our protestations of sincerity and intentions of decency, what concrete dikes are we erecting against the rising flood-tide of horror?

Orwell is writing a morality play which preaches the absolute truth that man is an end in himself. But while we may live always in quest of final judgment, we do exist in the *here and now*. Consequently our need is of some empirical judgments that can state with *some* certainty the consequences of an action. Is, for example, the action of the British Labor government in creating a wage freeze the imposition of controls whose consequence is the acceleration of power concentration and the total state? Or is the creation of the central intelligence agency in the U.S.—voted recently by Congress—with the power to plant agents in every voluntary association in the country, including trade unions, another step toward that end? Are not these irreversible steps, and hence, the danger that we are being warned against?

What are the safeguards and the checks? Tradition? Intelligent citizenship? Democratic awareness? Participation? Are these enough when power is at stake? Professor Harold Lasswell, in his book *Power and Personality,* has proposed a National Personal Assessment Board, a democratic elite of skill, to devise and administer personality tests that would weed out

those obsessed with power. And Dr C. S. Bluemel, a psychiatrist, in his *War, Politics and Insanity* would limit the suffrage right to university graduates who had majored in the social sciences and who had been certified as free of personality disorders by the faculty. At this point, sanity itself teeters on the balance, the obsessive fear arises and as the prophet Micah concludes, in Morton Wishengrad's fable of the *Thief and the Hangman,* 'when society plays the hangman, who is the hangman's hangman.'
 —Daniel Bell, "Utopian Nightmare," *New Leader,* 25 June 1949, p. 8

ALDOUS HUXLEY ON *BRAVE NEW WORLD* AND *NINETEEN EIGHTY-FOUR*

[Aldous Huxley (1894–1963) was a prolific British novelist whose dystopia, *Brave New World* (1932), may have influenced *Nineteen Eighty-Four.* In this letter to Orwell, Huxley makes several comparisons between Orwell's novel and his own, suggesting that his work is more plausible in its predictions of the future.]

The philosophy of the ruling majority in *Nineteen Eighty-Four* is a sadism which has been carried to its logical conclusion by going beyond sex and denying it. Whether in actual fact the policy of the boot-on-the-face can go on indefinitely seems doubtful. My own belief is that the ruling oligarchy will find less arduous and wasteful ways of governing and satisfying its lust for power, and that these ways will resemble those which I described in *Brave New World.* ⟨. . .⟩ Within the next generation I believe that the world's rulers will discover that infant conditioning and narco-hypnosis are more efficient, as instruments of government, than clubs and prisons, and that the lust for power can be just as completely satisfied by suggesting people into loving their servitude as by flogging and kicking them into obedience. In other words, I feel that the nightmare of *Nineteen Eighty-Four* is destined to modulate into the night-

mare of a world having more resemblance to that which I imagined in *Brave New World.* The change will be brought about as a result of a felt need for increased efficiency. Meanwhile, of course, there may be a large-scale biological and atomic war—in which case we shall have nightmares of other and scarcely imaginable kinds.
—Aldous Huxley, Letter to George Orwell (21 October 1949), *Letters of Aldous Huxley,* ed. Grover Smith (London: Chatto & Windus, 1969), pp. 604–5

STEPHEN SPENDER ON EVIL IN *NINETEEN EIGHTY-FOUR*

[Stephen Spender (b. 1909) is one of the most distinguished British critics of the century. Among his critical works are *The Destructive Element* (1935), *Love-Hate Relations: A Study of Anglo-American Sensibilities* (1974), and *The Thirties and After* (1978). He is also a respected poet, and he has recently published his autobiography, *World within World* (1994). In this extract, Spender notes that, although Orwell could not find in religion a solution to the political problems he outlined in *Nineteen Eighty-Four,* his conception of Big Brother is a kind of Antichrist figure.]

⟨. . .⟩ for Orwell no return either to tradition or to religion is possible. If society cannot be saved, he is scarcely interested in saving himself from society, and if it is damned, then he pins hope not to his own art or soul but to the unpolitical recklessness of the 'proles'. He was a man more deeply concerned with the political future of society than with his own life or work, though he did not believe, at the end, that any political solution was possible. ⟨. . .⟩

In *1984* there has been a purging by Orwell of simplified political good-and-evil, parallel to Eliot's. In the end Big Brother and his Party are not bad because they are politically reactionary or even totalitarian, but because they indulge a lust

33

for power which approaches very nearly to a lust for pure evil. And as in Baudelaire's Paris, the highest possible good in the conditions of *1984* has become a conscious pursuit of sensuality. For where good is impossible, the sins of the senses can be used as a moral weapon against abstract evil. *1984* is a political novel in which politics have been completely purged of current assumptions such as that the Left is good and the Right bad. We are confronted with a world in which any side can use politics as an excuse for plunging the world in evil.

And although there is no Christ in Orwell's world, Big Brother is really anti-Christ. He wills that the whole society shall will nothing except his will, he demands the love of his victims, in their lives and in the manner of their deaths. If the idea of the equality of man is the centre of Orwell's abandoned vision, the idea of the will of Big Brother is the centre of his anti-vision. Thus as we read on we realize that those slogans introduced at the beginning of the book, which at first read like crude parodies, are literally the moral laws of a world where Evil has become the anti-Christ's Good. LOVE IS HATE, WAR IS PEACE, AND IGNORANCE IS STRENGTH are the basic principles of belief for the members of the Inner Party, and Winston Smith experiences a feeling of conversion when he is completely convinced that a lie is the truth. He loves Big Brother.

The tragedy of Orwell's novel is that man—Big Brother—turns himself into God, but there is no God.
—Stephen Spender, *The Creative Element: A Study of Vision, Despair and Orthodoxy among Some Modern Writers* (London: Hamish Hamilton, 1953), pp. 137–38

IRVING HOWE ON ORWELL AND TOTALITARIANISM

[Irving Howe (1920–1993) was one of the leading literary and cultural critics of the century. He wrote many books, including *Politics and the Novel* (1957), *The Critical Point: On Literature and Culture* (1973), and

World of Our Fathers (1976). In this extract, Howe notes that Orwell's success in depicting a totalitarian state in *Nineteen Eighty-Four* was in exercising his imagination in extrapolating the future from the present realities.]

Orwell's profoundest insight is that in a totalitarian world man's life is shorn of dynamic possibilities. The end of life is completely predictable in its beginning, the beginning merely a manipulated preparation for the end. There is no opening for surprise, for that spontaneous animation which is the token of and justification for freedom. Oceanic society may evolve through certain stages of economic development, but the life of its members is static, a given and measured quantity that can neither rise to tragedy nor tumble to comedy. Human personality, as we have come to grasp for it in a class society and hope for it in a classless society, is obliterated; man becomes a function of a process he is never allowed to understand or control. The fetishism of the state replaces the fetishism of commodities.

There have, of course, been unfree societies in the past, yet in most of them it was possible to find an oasis of freedom, if only because none had the resources to enforce total consent. But totalitarianism, which represents a decisive break from the Western tradition, aims to permit no such luxuries; it offers a total "solution" to the problems of the twentieth century, that is, a total distortion of what might be a solution. To be sure, no totalitarian state has been able to reach this degree of "perfection," which Orwell, like a physicist who in his experiment assumes the absence of friction, has assumed for Oceania. But the knowledge that friction can never actually be absent does not make the experiment any less valuable.

To the degree that the totalitarian state approaches its "ideal" condition, it destroys the margin for unforeseen behavior; as a character in Dostoevsky's *The Possessed* remarks, "Only the necessary is necessary." Nor is there a social crevice in which the recalcitrant or independent mind can seek shelter. The totalitarian state assumes that—given modern technology, complete political control, the means of terror and a rationalized contempt for moral tradition—anything is possible. Anything can be done with men, anything with their minds, with history and with words. Reality is no longer something to be acknowledged or experienced or even transformed; it is fabricated according to the need and will of the state, sometimes in anticipation of the future, sometimes as a retrospective improvement upon the past.

But even as Orwell, overcoming the resistance of his own nausea, evoked the ethos of the totalitarian world, he used very little of what is ordinarily called "imagination" in order to show how this ethos stains every aspect of human life. Like most good writers, he understood that imagination is primarily the capacity for apprehending reality, for seeing more clearly and deeply whatever it is that exists. That is why his vision of social horror, if taken as a model rather than a portrait, strikes one as essentially credible, while the efforts of most writers to create utopias or anti-utopias founder precisely on their desire to be scientific or inventive. Orwell understood that social horror consists not in the prevalence of diabolical machines or in the invasion of Martian automatons flashing death rays from mechanical eyes, but in the persistence of inhuman relations among men.

And he understood, as well, the significance of what I can only call the psychology and politics of "one more step." From a bearable neurosis to a crippling psychosis, from a decayed society in which survival is still possible to a totalitarian state in which it is hardly desirable, there may be only "one step." But it is decisive and, for all we know, irrevocable. To lay bare the logic of that social regression which leads to totalitarianism, Orwell had merely to allow his imagination to take . . . one step.
—Irving Howe, "Orwell: History as Nightmare," *American Scholar* 25, No. 2 (Spring 1956): 197–99

A. E. Dyson on *Nineteen Eighty-Four* as the Culmination of Orwell's Career

[A. E. Dyson (b. 1928) is a distinguished British critic and author of *The Crazy Fabric: Essays in Irony* (1965) and, with Julian Lovelock, *Masterful Images: English Poetry from Metaphysicals to Romantics* (1976). He is a former senior lecturer in English and American studies at the University of East Anglia. In this extract, Dyson notes that *Nineteen Eighty-Four* embodies many of the themes found in Orwell's previous works, notably a yearning for social justice, doubt of humanity's ability to defeat evil, and distrust of intellectuals.]

1984 is best approached by the way of the early Orwell, rather than as a phenomenon on its own. Sir Richard Rees has discerned in Orwell, in his recent excellent biography, four apparently contrasting strains: the rebel, the paternalist, the rationalist and the romantic. He has reminded us that Orwell was a man in whom a passionate desire for justice and a passionately bitter pessimism were always apt to meet. Possibly in some sense this could be said of all major satirists, but in Orwell the conjunction seems especially close. His anger is curiously poised between the constructive and the negative. There is genuine hope for moral improvement in men as a realisable ideal, and genuine fear that such improvement may be incompatible with human nature as it is. The hero of *Keep the Aspidistra Flying* is a fairly obvious example of a man in whom anger begins in hope, but ends in blackness and despair. He rages against hypocrisy and cant, and the ideal he fights for—a more egalitarian, more vital humanity—would be acknowledged by many great rebels of the modern world. But this idealistic anger readily merges into something very different from itself, an 'evil mutinous mood', to use Orwell's own term. Self-pity and laziness, cruelty and despair tinge and colour the anger, until it becomes an insupportable burden to the hero himself, and to everyone he is concerned with. Notoriously, anger is the chameleon emotion, changing colour and mood unnoticed, and very subtly allowing the best in a man to offer sanctions to the worst. The uniqueness of Orwell's anger is that he was entirely conscious of these dangers, as he shows in this fairly early work, yet entirely unable to escape from their implications. His consciousness of the worst that can happen, both for one individual man and for humanity, was almost obsessive. The worst enforced itself upon him as more powerful, because more plausible than the best: indeed, as more powerful because more plausible than the second-best, in so far as this can be equated with a world of mixed good and evil, guilt and expiation in which most men conceive their lot. His anger becomes, at such times, his awareness of life itself. One can no longer distinguish it from a grim sense of some hostile inevitability, against which moral idealism is fated to wrestle in vain.

In the early Orwell as well as in the later, one sees side by side with pure ideals of justice and humanity this pure doubt about whether men are capable of achieving such ideals. It is not only his attitude to the working class that is notoriously ambivalent, but almost equally his attitude to that smaller class to which he himself reluctantly belonged: the well-educated, middle-class intellectuals, aspiring to intelligent committal and goodwill in an increasingly chaotic world. The working-class characters in his early novels may not be as grotesquely inadequate as the sheep in *Animal Farm* or the proles in *1984,* but they offer little social hope for the rational mind. In the same way, the real-life intellectuals of the '30s may have been less systematically corrupt than Napoleon or O'Brien, but in Orwell's eyes they were no trustworthy architects of a better world.

He had, in fact, a very English dislike of intellectuals, suspecting that anyone willing to wear such a label would be diminished and depraved by it. He mistrusted the utopian aspirations of many left-wingers, feeling that behind their true radical decency there was a fatal failure to *see.* What did they fail to see? Partly, that pacifism was parasitic on exactly the forces and people it scorned (he quotes with approval Kipling's famous jibe, against those who mock 'the uniforms that guard you while you sleep'); partly, that an élite mentality can be both arrogant and unrealistic in assessing its own importance to the world. Most of all, however, he thought the left-wing idealists failed to see those evil forces of which he was almost as conscious in his early life as when he came to write *1984*: the harsh realities of power, underlying parties of the left as well as of the right, and making any simple formula of good versus evil dangerously trivial and naïve.
   —A. E. Dyson, "Orwell: Irony as Prophecy," *The Crazy Fabric: Essays in Irony* (London: Macmillan, 1965), pp. 200–202

George Woodcock on Orwell and Family Life

[George Woodcock (b. 1912) is a leading Canadian critic and author. Among his many books are *The Canadians* (1979), *Strange Bedfellows: The State and the Arts in Canada* (1985), and *Oscar Wilde: The Double Image* (1989). In this extract from his book on Orwell, Woodcock maintains that Orwell, although he himself never married, saw in the family a bulwark against social and political repression.]

Orwell may have been in respects a solitary, but in his eyes the family was important for the health of society and the fulfillment of the individual. Although he wrote a great deal about the unhappiness of his childhood, it is significant that even in his melancholy work *Such, Such Were the Joys,* he remembered his home as "a place ruled by love rather than fear." Whatever wounds his childhood may have given him, they did not deprive him of the desire to found a family himself, and he took a great pleasure in his adoptive parenthood. But this was one of the aspects of his life about which Orwell was reticent, and I will trespass on it no further, since beyond a certain point one inevitably becomes entangled in conjecture. Turning to his works rather than his life, it is significant that two of his novels, *Keep the Aspidistra Flying* and *Coming Up for Air,* end right in the heart of the family, with the prodigal heroes returning to take their medicine, and that one of the most unpleasant aspects of the Utopian society which Orwell stresses in *Nineteen Eighty-Four* is the shattering of family trust by turning children into spies against their parents.

At a time when apologies for the family were almost entirely the work of Catholic writers, Orwell's attitude was, here again, exceptional for a left-wing intellectual, but there is no doubt of the genuineness of his feeling that anything which threatened the family or interfered with the natural process of increase was an almost blasphemous attack on life itself. In *Nineteen Eighty-Four,* the Party pries into the sexual lives of its members and even runs an Anti-Sex League (successor of the birth-control organizations which Orwell detested in his own day), but the proles carry on their sexual life without any restraint except that imposed by their own moral code. The proles are in this

way also the successors of the early twentieth-century working class whom Orwell admired for their lack of middle-class puritanism; in "The Art of Donald McGill" he observed how robustly they jested about sex, but also how they approved only those sexual relations that led in the right direction, towards marriage well blessed with children. At the same time, in their jokes and songs, they celebrated the sexual act and the fertility deities, the mother of goddesses, who appeared in comic modern disguise on the postcards which formed their most popular art.
—George Woodcock, *The Crystal Spirit: A Study of George Orwell* (Boston: Little, Brown, 1966), pp. 262–63

RAYMOND WILLIAMS ON ORWELL, TOTALITARIANISM, AND CAPITALISM

[Raymond Williams (1921–1988), a fellow of Jesus College, Cambridge, was a leading British leftist critic of literature, drama, and society. Among his many books are *The Country and the City* (1973), *Culture and Society 1780–1950* (1983), and *The Politics of Modernism* (1989). In this extract from his monograph on Orwell, Williams observes that Orwell's obsession with totalitarianism blinded him to the comparable evils to be found in other political systems, notably militaristic capitalism.]

His vision of power politics is also close and convincing. The transposition of official "allies" and "enemies" has happened, almost openly, in the generation since he wrote. His idea of a world divided into three blocs—Oceania, Eurasia, and Eastasia, of which two are always at war with the third though the alliances change—is again too close for comfort. And there are times when one can believe that what "had been called England or Britain" has become simply Airstrip One.

With these elements of the projection so recognizable, at least in their general outlines, it is necessary to ask why so much else is so wrong. It is significant that Orwell took his model of a controlled and military society from Soviet communism, even including detailed elements of its past such as the conflict between Stalin and Trotsky (Big Brother and Goldstein). The ideology of Airstrip One is Ingsoc—English socialism—and when the book became a success in the United States he had to issue a denial that this related to the postwar Labour government:

> My recent novel is NOT intended as an attack on Socialism or on the British Labour Party (of which I am a supporter) but as a show-up of the perversions to which a centralised economy is liable and which have already been partly realised in Communism and Fascism.

Ingsoc, it might then be said, is no more English socialism than Minitrue is the Ministry of Truth. But the identification was in effect made, and it was profoundly damaging. Not in what it said about Soviet society—Orwell's position there was clear and consistent—but in what it implied generally about socialism and a "centralised economy." This connects with the most evident error in Orwell's projection: that the permanent and controlled war economy is shabby and undersupplied. The structural relations that we have since seen between a militarist economy and a controlled consumer affluence amount to more than a historical development that Orwell did not foresee. They indicate some of the social facts that, in what became an obsession with ideology, he did not take account of. There are good reasons why Orwell might not have foreseen an affluent and militaristic capitalism, or a world of international corporations that functioned, internally and externally, very much like his projected Party. But he had the best of reasons—in direct experience—to know that political police, for example, were not a socialist or communist invention; or propaganda, or censorship, or *agents provocateurs.* By assigning all modern forms of repression and authoritarian control to a single political tendency, he not only misrepresented it but cut short the kind of analysis that would recognize these inhuman and destructive forces wherever they appeared, under whatever names and masked by whatever ideology. For it would certainly, now, be *doublethink* to suppose that the only source of these elements is a form of socialism, just as only *thoughtcrime* could prevent

us from seeing a propaganda phrase like "the free world" as a very clear example of Newspeak. In projecting an all too recognizable world Orwell confused us about its structures, its ideologies, and the possibilities of resisting it.
 — Raymond Williams, *George Orwell* (New York: Columbia University Press, 1971), pp. 76–78

Gorman Beauchamp on Sexuality as a Form of Political Defiance

[Gorman Beauchamp (b. 1938) is the author of *Jack London* (1984) and the coeditor of *Utopian Studies 1* (1987). He is a professor of English at the University of Michigan. In this extract, Beauchamp notes that *Nineteen Eighty-Four* bears many similarities to E. I. Zamiatin's *We,* particularly in the way in which sexuality is used as a means of political defiance.]

The influence of Zamiatin's work on *1984* is pronounced and pervasive; indeed, one critic has called *We* Orwell's *Holinshed.* Many of the features of the United State reappear in Orwell's Oceania, not least of which is the systematic repression of the sexual drives. Thus the rebellion of the individual against the State, in *1984* as in *We,* is presented as a sexual one, the struggle for instinctual freedom against the enforced conformity of an omniscient, omnipotent *étatisme.* Orwell's Winston Smith, like Zamiatin's D-503, is the last Adam, reenacting the myth of the Fall, following his Eve into disobedience against God.

 The topography of Oceania is well enough known that I need not dwell on it: the telescreens, Big Brother's electronic eyes that are always "watching you"; the phenomena of *newspeak* and *doublethink* and *blackwhite;* the ubiquitous slogans proclaiming war to be peace and freedom slavery. Nor need I stress the dystopian nature of Orwell's vision of utopia at dead end, all its perverted values terroristically enforced by the Ministry of Love. What should be pointed out, however, is the remarkably precise way in which Orwell has embodied, in the conditioned hysteria of love for Big Brother, Freud's theory of eroticism displaced. In the daily Two-Minute Hate (the Oceanic equivalent of prayer), the telescreens project the image of Goldstein, the satan of this State, against whom the increasingly frenzied faithful hurl their hatred. Then (Winston recounts of one such Hate) "drawing a sigh of relief from everybody, the hostile figure melted into the face of Big Brother . . . full of power and mysterious calm, and so vast that it filled the screen. . . . The little sandy-haired woman had flung herself over the chair in front of her. With a tremendous murmur that sounded like 'My savior!' she extended her arms to the screen." Julia, Winston's Eve, explains "the inner meaning of the Party's sexual puritanism."

> It was not merely that the sex instinct created a world of its own which was outside the Party's control and which therefore had to be destroyed if possible. What was more important was that sexual privation induced hysteria, which was desirable because it could be transformed into war fever and hero worship. The way she put it was:
> "When you make love you're using up energy; and afterwards you feel happy and don't give a damn for anyone. They can't bear you to feel like that. They want you to be bursting with energy all the time. All this marching up and down and cheering and waving flags is simply sex gone sour. If you're happy inside yourself, why should you get excited about Big Brother?"

In order to ensure that the Oceanians *do* get excited about Big Brother—displace, that is, eroticism from its natural object, another individual, to the State—the Party attempts in every way "to remove all pleasure from the sex act. . . . The only recognized purpose of marriage was to beget children for the service of the Party. Sexual intercourse was to be looked on as a slightly disgusting operation, like having an enema." Thus the Party instigated organizations like the Junior Anti-Sex League, a sort of celibate Scouts, whose chastity, like that of medieval monks and nuns, demonstrated their superior love for and loyalty to their god. For the Party's ultimate aim, as the Inquisitorial figure O'Brien explains to Winston, is the total abolition of the sex instinct: "We shall abolish the orgasm. Our neurologists are at work upon it now. . . There will be no love,

except love for Big Brother." Even more clearly than in Zamiatin's United State, the rulers of Oceania have grasped the threat to utopianism posed by man's sexuality and are moving drastically to destroy or displace it.
—Gorman Beauchamp, "Of Man's Last Disobedience: Zamiatin's We and Orwell's *1984*," *Comparative Literature Studies* 10, No. 4 (December 1973): 293–94

WILLIAM STEINHOFF ON ORWELL AND JAMES BURNHAM

[William Steinhoff (b. 1914), a former professor of English at the University of Michigan, is the author of *George Orwell and the Origins of* 1984 (1975), from which the following extract is taken. Here, Steinhoff believes that Orwell was significantly influenced by the British political thinker James Burnham in his portrayal of a future society in *Nineteen Eighty-Four*.]

If one had to choose a single writer who most profoundly affected the shaping of *1984,* that writer would, I believe, be James Burnham. His arguments about the nature of the changes taking place in modern society as well as the way Orwell responded to them and their development and alteration in Burnham's later work have already been discussed. Some of Burnham's ideas were, as we saw, accepted by Orwell: the concentration of industry and hence of its control, the erosion of capitalist ideology and morale, the rise of a class of managers to replace the owner-capitalists, the emergence of superstates, and the potential perversion of the ideal of socialism. He rejected other ideas: Burnham's theory of power and what Orwell called his "power-worship," as well as many of Burnham's predictions, including his belief that a preventive war against the Soviet Union was inevitable.

What Orwell has done in *1984* is to assume that Burnham's analysis is correct and to work out the consequences. As he said, "James Burnham's theory has been much discussed, but few people have yet considered its ideological implications—that is, the kind of world-view, the kind of beliefs, and the social structure that would probably prevail in a State which was at once *unconquerable* and in a permanent state of war with its neighbours." We know that Orwell disagreed profoundly with many of Burnham's beliefs, but there is no overt sign of this disagreement in the novel and no reason why there should be. Like "A Modest Proposal," *1984* assumes the existence of certain conditions and certain tendencies of mind and attempts to work out their outrageous consequences in order to effect in the reader a revulsion against them.

Emmanuel Goldstein's *The Theory and Practice of Oligarchical Collectivism*—the Book—is in style and content inspired by Burnham's *The Managerial Revolution* and *The Machiavellians*. Deutscher claims, however, that the fragments of the Book "are an obvious, though not very successful, paraphrase of Trotsky's *The Revolution Betrayed.*" Presumably this opinion rests on the identification of Goldstein with Trotsky, which Orwell acknowledged, for Deutscher offers no evidence to support it. Trotsky's book describes how, after the death of Lenin, the aims and methods of the revolution were perverted as Stalin gradually consolidated his power. With a wealth of statistics and details it concentrates on Russian developments. It is thus not mainly a theoretical treatise, nor is it, like Burnham's books, a comprehensive study of world politics or human motives. There are indeed similarities in style between Burnham and Trotsky; the tone of the authority which they have in common is especially noticeable. But even in its style Goldstein's book has greater similarities to Burnham's, since Burnham is not impeded by the necessity to detail events that have already taken place, and consequently his language and manner can be more sweeping and assured. Furthermore, the Book deals with some subjects treated explicitly by Burnham but not Trotsky. ⟨. . .⟩

The point of greatest difference between Burnham and Orwell lies in their attitude toward power and its use. In *1984* all the questions implicit in this subject are concentrated in the entry Winston Smith makes in his diary: *"I understand HOW; I do not understand WHY."* Later on, when he is being brainwashed and is compelled by O'Brien to speculate about

"WHY?" he replies in his old-fashioned way, "You are ruling over us for our own good. . . . You believe that human beings are not fit to govern themselves, and therefore—" a mistake punished by an electric shock. O'Brien tells him what he should have said, "The Party seeks power entirely for its own sake. We are not interested in the good of others; we are interested solely in power."

Two questions may be asked about O'Brien's statement. First, did Orwell himself believe this to be a satisfactory explanation of why some men act as they do? And second, is it a reasonable opinion? Orwell did indeed think—and with reason—that some men hunger to have power over others; but, as we know, that is not all he believed. To assume that O'Brien's answer to Winston Smith's implied question is what Orwell himself would have said is to misread *1984*.

O'Brien's answer echoes Burnham's thesis in *The Machiavellians*. The passage in which Orwell himself specifically rejected Burnham's thesis, in an article in the *Manchester Evening News*, is worth repeating: "It would seem that the theory that there is no such thing as a 'good' motive in politics, that nothing counts except force and fraud, has a hole in it somewhere, and that the Machiavellian system fails, even by its own test of material success."
—William Steinhoff, *George Orwell and the Origins of* 1984 (Ann Arbor: University of Michigan Press, 1975), pp. 200–201, 203

Lillian Feder on Language and Selfhood in *Nineteen Eighty-Four*

[Lillian Feder, a former professor of English and comparative literature at Queens College and the Graduate Center of the University of New York, has written *Ancient Myth in Modern Poetry* (1971) and *Madness in Literature* (1980). In this extract, Feder points out that

Winston Smith's diary is his attempt to preserve his selfhood in a repressive political environment.]

Early in *Nineteen Eighty-Four,* "the last man," as Orwell calls him, begins a diary "for the future, for the unborn." A little later, acknowledging that the diary will no doubt be "vaporized" along with himself and that the time he addresses may be "imaginary," he nonetheless expands his potential audience *To the future or to the past, to a time when thought is free. . . ."* Although he writes in a panic, aware that keeping a record of his thoughts and activities is an offense punishable by death, Winston Smith is not yet conscious of the exact nature of the most serious crime he is committing against the state of Oceania: the use of language in the act of self-creation.

Nineteen Eighty-Four has been discussed from many points of view: as an attack on Soviet communism (or, more specifically, on the British Labour Party), as a defense of bourgeois society, as a revelation of Orwell's paranoia, as a prophecy of worldwide totalitarianism through absolute control of the human mind, and as a study of the psychology of submission. Some of these interpretations now seem dated, either because they reflect political alliances of a certain period in history or because they convey a rather naïve approach to the connection between an author's biography and his work; and even those which consider the book on its own terms seem to miss its deepest revelations both for the time in which it appeared and for the present. *Nineteen Eighty-Four* does not simply satirize a totalitarian state forcing human beings to capitulate to its demands through propaganda, deprivation, and torture. Its continuous prophetic meaning lies in its revelation of the individual's biological and psychological resistance to his own adaptation to political and social constraints. The major conflict of this novel centers around selfhood, the struggle over unconscious and conscious mental processes between a solitary man and the united forces of international oppression.

Relying on the only resources he has—dreams, memories of beauty, love, and sorrow, and fragments of history—Winston Smith tries to apprehend the intrinsic connection between selfhood, language, and objective reality. It is an issue we are still confronting. In fact, Smith's struggle for selfhood is a prophetic illumination of two important cultural problems of the present that are deeply related: first, the steady extinction of precision and elegance of language and the consequent poverty of expression in speech and imaginative writing; and second, the estrangement of currently fashionable literary criticism, particularly deconstruction, from the reality that literature incorporates and re-creates. Inarticulateness, involuntary or contrived, indicates ignorance of or disrespect for cultural history; deconstruction assumes its own ahistorical authority. Furthermore, both these products of contemporary culture, different as they may seem, reveal an inadequate comprehension of the physiological and psychological complexity of selfhood and its simultaneous identification with and opposition to the political and social environment in which it is continually created. The distrust of the ego and the preference for psychic adventurism expressed in much contemporary literature find their critical counterpart in Roland Barthes's notion of a "text of bliss" which is "outside criticism, *unless it is reached through another text of bliss.*" The commentator on such a text can "only . . . enter into a desperate plagiarism" with it, and thus "hysterically affirm the void of bliss." ⟨. . .⟩

I cannot agree with Irving Howe's view that "Orwell has imagined a world in which the self, whatever subterranean existence it manages to eke out, is no longer a significant value, not even a value to be violated." The seven years that O'Brien, a leading member of the inner Party, spends in surveillance of Smith and the time and effort he invests in interrogating and torturing him until his ultimate surrender of selfhood indicate quite the opposite: the self is the greatest challenge to a totalitarian regime's authorized versions of reality; it is to be eradicated not only by imprisonment and physical abuse but by the conversion of language and culture into mental barriers. Orwell charts the conflicting psychological reactions of his protagonist: awareness of inhibition, resistance, conflict, expression of impulses, compromise, and finally the absolute denial of the very processes of selfhood.

In so doing, Orwell does not develop traditional fictional characters; Winston Smith is a prototype of man deliberately being remade by political and technological forces, the state's evidence that not only culture but human biology and psychology are its antagonists and its conquests. Thus, whereas the reader does not respond to Smith as a multifaceted individual, he does enter into his mental and psychological contest, which constitutes the self in its ultimate struggle against suppression and disintegration.

—Lillian Feder, "Selfhood, Language, and Reality: George Orwell's *Nineteen Eighty-Four,*" *Georgia Review* 37, No. 2 (Summer 1983): 392–94

PAUL R. EHRLICH AND ANNE H. EHRLICH ON ORWELL AND POPULATION

[Paul R. Ehrlich (b. 1932), Bing Professor of Biological Sciences at Stanford University, and Anne H. Ehrlich (b. 1933), a senior research associate at Stanford University, have cowritten several books on population and the environment, including *The End of Affluence* (1974), *The Population Explosion* (1990), and *Healing the Planet* (1991). In this extract, the Ehrlichs note that Orwell's failure to predict the population explosion following World War II have produced conditions totally different from those envisioned in *Nineteen Eighty-Four*.]

The analysis of the environmental aspects of *Nineteen Eighty-Four* that follows is in several respects unfair to George Orwell. Anyone who writes about the future knows that precise prediction is impossible. One can forecast the implications of current trends on the assumption that they will continue; but the forecaster is always aware that many trends are unlikely to continue. We would view *Nineteen Eighty-Four* as a *scenario,* a device used to stimulate thinking about the future implications of the present course of society. In that context it was an enormous success, for, whether it was intended as a forecast or a warning, *Nineteen Eighty-Four* alerted people to certain dehumanizing trends—some of which still seem very threatening today—flowing partly from technological advances.

What struck us most sharply, however, upon reading *Nineteen Eighty-Four* for its treatment of environmental issues was not Orwell's prescience in this area, but his blindness. In this particular context he was completely a man of his times. But that the same blindness should still afflict many educated people today is frightening. These people have little excuse for their affliction; unlike George Orwell, they live in a society where information on environmental issues is widely available. Environmental blindness allows people to imagine humanity as abstracted from nature and affected only by social phenomena, answerable only to itself and to the gods of its invention. Partly because of this blindness, Orwell's fictional world, created just after World War II, is a poor reflection of the real world today.

A major theme in *Nineteen Eighty-Four* is the use of perpetual warfare by the Party, not just to generate a continuous war hysteria and thereby manipulate the citizenry more easily, but also to avoid the surpluses that would inevitably be created if peace were to reign. This policy is explicitly stated: "The primary aim of modern warfare . . . is to use up the products of the machine without raising the general standard of living. . . . If the machine were used deliberately for that end, hunger, overwork, illiteracy, and disease could be eliminated within a few generations."

Orwell here appears to have embedded a local partial truth in a global misperception. It is true that one function of military expenditure in either war or peace in real "steel-eating" societies is to accelerate the conversion of natural resources to rubbish—to boost the economy by speeding up throughout. But whether this function could legitimately be called primary, and whether it is ever consciously planned for the purpose of keeping the general standard of living low, are much more problematic.

The operative global misperception is that past triumphs of "the machine" indicate that it has a capacity, in essence, to solve permanently all problems for a human population of indefinite size. This misperception—based in ignorance of physics, chemistry, and biology—is widespread in society even today, as evidenced by the writings of cornucopian economists. 〈. . .〉

There are, of course, some economists who understand that there are limits on what the machine can accomplish. But this view is as yet accepted by only a minority of the profession and probably of society as a whole. Orwell's mid-century picture of humanity as virtually disconnected from the physical and biological worlds is still all too persistent among the most influential of social scientists.

For much of Orwell's adult life, demographers were concerned that populations in the industrialized world might *decline*. It is not surprising, then, that Orwell paid scant attention to the problems of overpopulation. The demographic history of the thirty-five-year period between 1949, the year *Nineteen Eighty-Four* was published, and the approaching year 1984, has, of course, created conditions totally unlike those Orwell described. He indicated that the nation of Oceania—consisting of Britain, the Americas, Australasia (Australia and New Zealand, presumably), and southern Africa—have a 1984 population of about 300 million. This is actually well under the 1950 population of the Western Hemisphere alone, and far below the roughly 740 million people now living in that "nation."

Orwell's Oceania missed the post-World War II population explosion—arguably the most significant event of the era he was previewing. But there were good reasons why that explosion did not occur in Orwell's world. One was the decrease in reproduction achieved by the repression of sexual activity, as exemplified by the Junior Anti-Sex League. O'Brien states the goals of the Party: "Children will be taken from their mothers at birth, as one takes eggs from a hen. The sex instinct will be eradicated. Procreation will be an annual formality like the renewal of a ration card. We shall abolish the orgasm. . . . There will be no love, except the love of Big Brother."

Had Orwell been more scientifically oriented, he might have predicted that technological advances would make it possible, as indeed they have, to allow eggs to be taken from women and "hatched" elsewhere. Sex then could have been totally abolished in Oceania. The test-tube baby did not, however, originate in the societies (the Soviet Union and China) that most closely resemble that of *Nineteen Eighty-Four*. The

51

process was first perfected in richer, less repressed nations, not as a step toward state control of reproduction, but as a method of restoring fertility and gaining reproductive freedom.
—Paul R. Ehrlich and Anne H. Ehrlich, "1984: Population and Environment," *On* Nineteen Eighty-Four, ed. Peter Stansky (Stanford: Stanford Alumni Association, 1983), pp. 49–51

W. F. BOLTON ON ORWELL AND LANGUAGE

[W. F. Bolton (b. 1930) is a professor of English at Rutgers University. He has written *Shakespeare's English: Language in the History Plays* (1992), edited *The Middle Ages* (1987), and coedited *The English Language* (1987). In this extract from *The Language of 1984* (1984), Bolton believes that one of the chief features of *Nineteen Eighty-Four* and of Orwell's work in general is its emphasis on the connection between language and politics.]

Language stood in the foreground of George Orwell's mindscape. Though he called for social change, he felt keen nostalgia for the age he saw vanishing, and he felt change in language most keenly of all. Oppressed by the guilt he felt for his complicity in the British class system and the British Empire, he charted the barriers that dialect and language difference erected. In his literary criticism he made language a touchstone for good writing and for bad. He thought that literacy and the electronic media with their political and commercial blandishments threatened the subjugation, not the liberation, of the human mind.

Orwell's views of language permeate his writing from the earliest work onwards, but *Nineteen Eighty-Four* (1949) and the essay 'Politics and the English Language' (1946) characterize his outlook for most readers. Many who have never read him know the terminology of *Nineteen Eighty-Four*: 'doublethink' appears in college dictionaries for those who have not read Orwell's definition in the novel; 'Newspeak' became a dysphemism for utterances, notably in politics and advertising, much as 'fascism' had become a dysphemism for political systems (as Orwell observed). Though it is not Orwell's word, 'doublespeak' is transparently derived from 'doublethink' and 'Newspeak' (with the assistance from 'doubletalk'); and a *Dictionary,* and a *Quarterly Review,* of *Doublespeak* have appeared. The title of Orwell's last book has become a label for tyrannical invasion of privacy, just as 'Orwellian' (usually as an adjective modifying 'nightmare') has become shorthand for ruthless oppression. But the celebrity of his fictional future language should not conceal the range and complexity of the views on real and present language that he expressed elsewhere.

When he died, aged forty-six, from tuberculosis in 1950, Orwell had achieved international recognition: *Animal Farm* (1945) had been a critical and commercial success, resulting in the 1946 publication of his *Critical Essays*; and *Nineteen Eighty-Four* had been a Book-of-the-Month choice, reviewed in hundreds of journals from the *New Statesman* to *Life.* Orwell's literary reputation, and perhaps his early death, gave his linguistic views a currency they might not have had in other circumstances. 'Politics and the English Language' became a favorite text in American freshman English courses, and was anthologized in many freshman readers and 'taught' in hundreds of classrooms.

But the 'Politics' essay and *Nineteen Eighty-Four* did not simply gather lustre from Orwell's literary fame. Their influence came also from the activist political context in which he had set his linguistic views. Orwell's politics, which he described as 'democratic Socialist', were never party-line. His political views were widely compatible because they were broadly antitotalitarian. He hated all dogma, political included, preferring to see things as they were and to weigh them accordingly: Rosenfeld summarizes the usual view that 'Orwell was fair, honest, unassuming and reliable in everything he wrote'. But things as they were, and as he saw them, changed, as things and views do; so Orwell was not only independent but somewhat inconsistent. This is not a book about Orwell's politics as such, but his theory that language is a political force gives his politics a place here just the same. His political stance made him congenial to all but the most blimpish right and the most bolshevik left. Orwell, like the Dickens he wrote about, became 'one of those writers who are well worth stealing'. D.A.N. Jones poses, among his 'Arguments against Orwell', the fact that 'such writers as Robert Conquest and Kingsley Amis, who think themselves to be anti-Communists of Orwell's kind, . . . keenly support the American war . . . in Vietnam,' while at the same time 'two American leftists, Noam Chomsky and Norman Mailer, felt able to cite Orwell in support of their own position as opponents of their government's war policy.' Jones concludes, 'It seems that people of almost any political persuasion can find some of their beliefs expressed in Orwell's work, very eloquently.' No one except a few zealots would want to defend what Orwell attacked, and as the particulars of the scene he observed—Sir Stafford Cripps, Konni Zilliacus, and the rest—fade into historical distance, the generalities become even more congenial.

His linguistic views were part of that booty, adopted and repeated by many who could agree on little else. So Orwell is a favourite linguistic authority for politically conservative writers like Lincoln Barnett, who cited *Nineteen Eighty-Four* and quoted the 'Politics' essay with approval. At the same time he has the support of a political liberal like Arthur Schlesinger Jr, for whom 'the control of language is a necessary step toward the control of minds, as Orwell made so brilliantly clear in *1984*.' The vitality of Orwell's linguistic influence, then, has come not only from his wide literary influence, but from his broad political valence and the strong though vague connection between politics and the language that he proclaimed.

—W. F. Bolton, *The Language of* 1984: *Orwell's English and Ours* (Knoxville: University of Tennessee Press, 1984), pp. 15–17

LYNETTE HUNTER ON THE ENDING OF *NINETEEN EIGHTY-FOUR*

[Lynette Hunter, a senior lecturer in English at the University of Leeds in England, is the author of

G. K. Chesterton: Explorations in Allegory (1979), Rhetorical Stance in Modern Literature (1984), and Modern Allegory and Fantasy (1989). In this extract taken from her book on Orwell, Hunter focuses on the ending of Nineteen Eighty-Four, in which Winston Smith is finally broken and accepts Big Brother.]

The final chapter of Nineteen Eighty-Four illustrates Winston's total acceptance of O'Brien's system as it returns to the tempo of the earlier sections. But here the reader knows why Winston is inadequate and curiously it is also our own inadequacy. The analogy is carried by a reiteration of the image of the Chestnut Tree café. This final scene is an exact duplicate of the previous one in which Winston was searching for some radical or significant difference between his given world and actuality. There neither the reader nor Winston could interpret the scene, but here, after the process of the book which pulls the pieces together, and allows us to assess, Winston perceives nothing, while we do. We have taken on his discriminating role. The structure is again one of a dance, but here between Winston's thoughts and the interruptions of the telescreen. There is no longer even a generative conflict with O'Brien, but a controlled conflict with a false communicator. The game of chess he plays is associated with reports of war, both are conflicts as games. There are no real opponents, merely counters of established weight being moved around. We are told that in this chess game white always mates, and for the new Winston this is an emblem of the Party's omnipotence and perfection. The reader recognizes the falsity involved, and the contrast with Winston's earlier knowledge. When the telescreen announces victory, Winston realizes that it happened 'as he had foreseen' on the chess board. The coincidence of apparent reality with his own thoughts excites him enormously, as if he has finally participated in the game. He has been allowed to win, to control reality himself. The dance has ended.

Significantly, he can no longer distinguish between memory and reality, nor can he define reactions or values. 'Feeling', the earlier key to his standards, has been scrambled. Winston now responds with a 'violent emotion, not fear exactly but a sort of undifferentiated excitement'; or he has 'an extraordinary medley of feelings—but it was not a medley exactly; rather it was successive layers of feeling, in which one could not say which layer was uppermost . . .' He is left without an ability to differentiate in terms of value. Just as the image of chess presents its controlled quality of game alone, so the 'golden country' is fully realized and allowed only its controlled aspects of fulfilled desire and confession. Winston's final conversion leaves him:

> back in the ministry of love, with everything forgiven, his soul as white as snow . . . He was looking down the white-tiled corridor, with a feeling of walking in sunlight . . . The long-hoped-for bullet was entering his brain . . . He had won a victory over himself. He loved Big Brother.

All that is now left, having destroyed himself and achieved full acceptance is the desire for death. But whereas earlier death was either through private suffering or public extermination, Winston now looks on death not even as an active reward, but as the ultimate acceptance. The possibility of death being a positive act of contemplation is not even thought of.

Winston is now a useless bureaucrat who meets with others like himself to discuss notes to footnotes on obscure papers. These men have 'extinct eyes, like ghosts fading at cock-crow'. They are the dead in life, who come to life only when they hide their betrayals from themselves and fade back into corpses when they recognize them. In the same way Winston recognizes his betrayal of Julia and accepts it as an index of his inhumanity. The recognition triggers off the telescreen jeer, 'Under the spreading chestnut tree / I sold you and you sold me', and the tears well up in Winston's eyes as they did in Rutherford's, in the earlier café scene. There is an initial parallel that should make the reader read the image again: that betrayal should have such power to destroy means also that loyalty and trust must have some value. But further than this, what is questioned is why betrayal should have the value it does and similarly why its guilt should have the strength that it does.
  —Lynette Hunter, *George Orwell: The Search for a Voice* (Milton Keynes, UK: Open University Press, 1984), pp. 219–20

Daphne Patai on Women in *Nineteen Eighty-Four*

[Daphne Patai (b. 1943) is a professor in the women's studies program and the department of Spanish and Portuguese at the University of Massachusetts at Amherst. She has written several books on Brazilian writers as well as *The Orwell Mystique: A Study in Male Ideology* (1984), from which the following extract is taken. Here, Patai maintains that women in *Nineteen Eighty-Four* are always marginal characters, seen largely through the eyes of men.]

In the world of *Nineteen Eighty-Four,* although men fear women because they may be spies, in general the assumptions of male centrality and female "otherness" survive intact. Julia's love for Winston makes him healthier, whereas O'Brien's attentions destroy him physically and mentally, but Winston's true alliance, as we have seen, is with O'Brien, who engages him in combat and recognizes him as a worthy opponent—a recognition that means more to Winston than Julia's love.

The romance between Julia and Winston is far less important in the novel, and occupies less space, than the "romance" between Winston and O'Brien. This is clear from the novel's beginning when Winston fears and hates (because he desires) Julia while admiring and being drawn to O'Brien. In addition, Orwell devotes far more space to the details of Winston's torture than to the details of his affair with Julia. This affair is quite possibly a concession on Orwell's part to popular literature, as well as a vehicle for setting Winston's halfhearted rebellion in motion; but Winston's true longing is for intimacy with O'Brien, the most powerful man he knows. While Winston is never depicted in serious conversation with Julia, the talks with O'Brien that accompany Winston's torture and conversion are at the heart of the novel.

The minor role attributed to women in the novel cannot be interpreted as part of Orwell's strategy of criticizing and laying bare the dynamics of totalitarianism. As readers with a different kind of sensibility, we may be aware that *Nineteen Eighty-Four* depicts a masculinized world, but Orwell did not see it this way and never made any sort of critique of the sex-role system. Although there exists within the novel a certain amount of specific information about the Party's control over sexuality and family life, there is also a wealth of detail that merely demonstrates Orwell's habitual disdain for women, evident in all his work. Thus any analysis of sex roles in *Nineteen Eighty-Four* has to begin by distinguishing between Party policy toward Party women (the proles are ignored), as articulated in the novel, and Orwell's own attitudes that inadvertently seep into the text. ⟨. . .⟩

The women in Orwell's narrative by and large appear as caricatures: They are Party secretaries, Party fanatics, Party wives like Katharine or the stereotypically helpless housewife Mrs. Parsons. They are also antisex freaks or prole prostitutes. There is no woman character in the novel comparable to Syme or Charrington or O'Brien. Although Goldstein's book explains that the Inner Party is not linked by blood and that no racial discrimination is practiced—"Jews, Negroes, South Americans of pure Indian blood are to be found in the highest ranks of the Party"—no female Inner Party members are mentioned. When Winston sees a man and a woman in the canteen, he assumes that the woman is the man's secretary. In describing Julia's work in Pornosec (which churns out machine-produced pornographic literature for prole consumption), work that is assigned to unmarried girls because they are thought to be less vulnerable than men to the corrupting influences of pornography, Orwell includes the detail that "all the workers in Pornosec, except the heads of the departments, were girls." Although Orwell reveals male dominance to be a continuing feature of life in Oceania, he does not treat this as worthy of analysis and does not raise the issue of its role in a totalitarian society. Women's options in a given society, what access they have to earning their own living and what kind of living that would be compared, for example, to becoming a man's economic dependent in exchange for housework and child-care services; how, in general, society structures women's life paths in comparison with men's—all this has everything to do with the shape of life in that society. But Orwell does not realize this, judging by his lack of attention to this problem in *Nineteen*

Eighty-Four. Even Julia is a largely unexplored character, seen only in terms of her relationship with Winston.
—Daphne Patai, *The Orwell Mystique: A Study in Male Ideology* (Amherst: University of Massachusetts Press, 1984), pp. 239, 242–43

MARK CRISPIN MILLER ON *NINETEEN EIGHTY-FOUR* AND TELEVISION

[Mark Crispin Miller is a widely published authority on television and film. He is the author of *Boxed In: The Culture of TV* (1988) and the editor of *Seeing Through Movies* (1990). In this extract, Miller states that Winston Smith's state of mind at the end of the novel is disconcertingly similar to our own passive absorption of images and information from television.]

What is most disconcerting ⟨. . .⟩ about the ending of *Nineteen Eighty-Four* is not that Winston Smith has now been made entirely unlike us. In too many ways, the ex-hero of this brilliant, dismal book anticipates those TV viewers who are incapable of reading it: "In these days he could never fix his mind on any one subject for more than a few moments at a time." At this moment, Winston Smith is, for the first time in his life, not under surveillance. The motto, "Big Brother Is Watching You," is now untrue as a threat, as it has always been untrue as an assurance. And the reason why he is no longer watched is that the Oceanic gaze need no longer see through Winston Smith, because he is no longer "Winston Smith," but "a swirl of gritty dust," as primitive and transparent as the Party.

As this Smith slumps in the empty Chestnut Tree, credulously gaping, his ruined mind expertly jolted by the telescreen's managers, he signifies the terminal fulfillment of O'Brien's master-plan, which expresses the intentions not only of Orwell's fictitious Party, but of the corporate entity that, through TV, contains our consciousness today: "We shall squeeze you empty, and then we shall fill you with ourselves." The Party has now done for Winston Smith what all our advertisers want to do for us, and with our general approval—answer all material needs, in exchange for the self that might try to gratify them independently, and that might have other, subtler needs as well. As a consumer, in other words, Orwell's ex-hero really has it made. "There was no need to give orders" to the waiters in the Chestnut Tree. "They knew his habits." Furthermore, he "always had plenty of money nowadays." In short, the Party has paid him for his erasure with the assurance, "We do it *all* for you." And so this grotesque before-and-after narrative ends satirically as all ads end in earnest, with the object's blithe endorsement of the very product that has helped to keep him miserable: "But it was all right, everything was all right, the struggle was finished. He had won the victory over himself. He loved Big Brother."

It is a horrifying moment; but if we do no more than wince at it, and then forget about it, we ignore our own involvement in the horror, and thus complacently betray the hope that once inspired this vision. Surely Orwell would have us face the facts. Like Winston Smith, and like O'Brien and the others, we have been estranged from our desire by Enlightenment, which finally reduces all of its proponents into the blind spectators of their own annihilation. Unlike that Oceanic audience, however, the TV viewer does not gaze up at the screen with angry scorn or piety, but—perfectly enlightened—looks down on its images with a nervous sneer that cannot threaten them, but that only keeps the viewer himself from standing up. As you watch, there is no Big Brother out there watching you, not because there isn't a Big Brother, but because Big Brother is you, watching.

—Mark Crispin Miller, "Big Brother Is You, Watching," *Reflections on America, 1984: An Orwell Symposium,* ed. Robert Mulvihill (Athens: University of Georgia Press, 1986), pp. 197–98

Mark Connelly on Winston Smith and History

[Mark Connelly (b. 1951) is the author of *The Diminished Self* (1987), a study of Orwell from which the following extract is taken. Here, Connelly finds that Winston Smith's struggle to preserve his selfhood is guided by history and a search for the past.]

Smith's battle to retain his autonomy is largely historical. The novel opens with Smith committing the punishable offense of recording his impressions in a diary. His notebook is historical, a relic of a previous age, its pages some forty years old. Smith's alienation from history is dramatized when he considers the day's date. He feels "helpless" because he has no proof that it is actually 1984. In fact, he is only roughly sure of his own age. At the outset, Smith is unsure of his purpose. He sees himself writing to the future, for the unborn. Yet he senses futility in this mission because "either the future would resemble the present in which case it would not listen to him, or it would be different from it, and his predicament would be meaningless." Smith doubts his role as historian in a world where history is outlawed, when "not even an anonymous word scribbled on a piece of paper, could physically survive."

Yet Smith remains motivated to attempt an historical search, to communicate with the future, even if it costs him his life. He perceives himself to be a "lonely ghost" uttering truths no one would hear, but he senses that if he communicates he can maintain a sense of "continuity." Smith believes that "by staying sane" he can carry on "the human heritage." Writing in his diary, he addresses the unknown:

> To the future or to the past, to a time when thought is free, when men are different from one another and do not live alone—to a time when truth exists and what is done cannot be undone:
> From the age of uniformity, from the age of solitude, from the age of Big Brother, from the age of doublethink—greetings!

In making his historical search, Smith struggles to determine absolutes in a mutable world. "The Party told you to reject the evidence of your eyes and ears. . . . They were wrong and he was right. . . . The solid world exists, its laws do not change.

Stones are hard, water is wet, objects unsupported fall toward the earth's center."

Smith's search is supported by an event that occurred in 1973, when he possessed "after the event" evidence of falsification. "He had held it between his fingers for as long as thirty seconds." At work one day Smith came across a ten-year-old newspaper photograph of a party leader at a New York rally on a date when the leader was later accused of being on enemy soil. Like all enemies of the Party, the traitor "confesses" his crimes. Smith had concrete, historical evidence of falsehood:

> But this was concrete evidence; it was a fragment of the abolished past, like a fossil bone which turns up in the wrong stratum and destroys a geological theory. It was enough to blow the Party to atoms, if in some way it could have been published to the world and its significance made known.

Trapped in the superstate, under the ever-watching telescreen, Smith deposited the newspaper picture in the "memory hole" for incineration.

Searching for the past, Smith attempts to converse with an aged prole in a pub. Plying the eighty-year old man with beer, he attempts to verify or dismiss the Party version of the Revolution. The old man's memory is personal and fragmented, responding to a familiar word or phrase. Asked if life were better in 1925, the old man comments philosophically on his weak bladder. Smith sadly realizes the futility of this pursuit. Within a few decades no one will be able to provide a link to the past. Even now "oral history" is not possible "since the few scattered survivors from the ancient world were incapable of comparing one age with another."

Smith's search for the past leads him to return to the junk shop where he purchased his notebook. Here he buys a glass paperweight containing a bit of sea coral. "What appealed to him about it was not so much its beauty as the air it seemed to possess of belonging to an age quite different from the present one." Precious few relics of the past remain, most have been broken up and destroyed. Smith discovers a bookshelf in the store, but finds nothing of value. Pre-1960 books have long since been collected and destroyed. Even the landscape of London does not aid him in his search. "One could not learn

history from architecture any more than one could learn it from books. Statues, inscriptions, memorial stones, the names of streets—anything that might throw light upon the past had been systematically altered."
—Mark Connelly, *The Diminished Self: Orwell and the Loss of Freedom* (Pittsburgh: Duquesne University Press, 1987), pp. 51–54

PATRICK REILLY ON *NINETEEN EIGHTY-FOUR* AND MORAL CHOICE

[Patrick Reilly is the author of *George Orwell: The Age's Adversity* (1986), *The Literature of Guilt: From Gulliver to Golding* (1987), and *Lord of the Flies: Fathers and Sons* (1992). In this extract, taken from his book on *Nineteen Eighty-Four* (1989), Reilly observes that, although Winston Smith has been defeated at the end of the novel, Orwell is urging readers not to become like him and to retain our sense of personal responsibility and moral choice.]

We do Orwell a disservice in one of two equally fallacious ways. One is to see the undoubted despair and conclude that Orwell follows his text in surrendering to it; the other is to deny that there is any despair present to tempt either Orwell or ourselves. But Orwell neither quits nor placates; *Nineteen Eighty-Four* paradoxically continues to fight for man even as it depicts the destruction of the last man alive. Winston is doomed, and man within him, but we are not yet Winston, and, even in the pit of its pessimism, *Nineteen Eighty-Four* exhorts us not to become so. The text is summoning us to a struggle that is not yet lost. It is we, here and now, who will decide that outcome: Winston's future fate depends upon our present action.

This is, after all, the essence of the Judeo-Christian tradition of prophecy: it is always conditional, forever tied to human deeds and choices. If you eat this apple, you will lose Eden; if you battle onward, you will reach the Promised Land; if you do what is just, you will be saved. Otherwise, no. It all depends on you, your choosing, your doing. The woe foretold by the prophet will descend unless people change their ways: Nineveh, the great city, will be destroyed unless Jonah acts, and Nineveh listens. Orwell is the last of the prophets, the Jonah sent to us, and we would do well, as Nineveh did, to listen and repent.

Scrooge, carried to a churchyard by the Ghost of Christmas Yet to Come and motioned toward a grave, implores an answer to one question: " 'Are these the shadows of the things that Will be, or are they the shadows of things that May be, only?' " Scrooge concedes that certain courses of human action persevered in must produce certain results but begs to be told that " 'If the courses be departed from, the ends will change.' " It is the question that we inevitably put to *Nineteen Eighty-Four,* demanding of Orwell the nature of the shadows, ineluctable or contingent, cast by his dark book: is Oceania a fate or a warning? What will happen or what may, a solicitation to despair or a call to action? Satan in hell attempts to recruit the demoralized angels: "Awake, arise, or be for ever fallen!"—in vain, because hell is too late to recover. Oceania too is hell, but we are not yet in it, and Orwell employs Satan's summons to ensure that we never will be. Scrooge's question is answered: it is up to you.

Orwell is in our time the chief custodian of this tradition of human responsibility and moral choice. True, *Nineteen Eighty-Four* is "the last great book he happened to write before he happened to die." Yet it is also a kind of testament, however unwitting, the finely appropriate crown to a life of unremitting moral effort. Orwell dreamed of writing other books, and we mourn that he was not spared to do so. Yet, paradoxically, rather than a sense of loss there is a sense of completion, of a hero dead yet with his triumphs secured:

> Samson hath quit himself
> Like Samson, and heroicly hath finished
> A life heroic.

Nothing is here for tears. Of course, his last book is profoundly disturbing in that it demolishes our ignorance and our alibi together. We now know that we are responsible, and the closer Oceania comes, the guiltier we are. But this book of destruction can also be our means of salvation, and if we do save ourselves, we should remember our chief benefactor. Without minimizing the threat or underestimating the danger, we must believe (but not too easily) that we can foil Oceania. That is the human response and is surely the one that Orwell sought. When we are finally safe, we should do homage for our deliverance to this fiercest tocsin of the twentieth century; it would be a shabby recompense if future generations, untroubled in their freedom, were to find *Nineteen Eighty-Four* only the hysteria of a neurotic panic-monger, ungratefully unaware of the unbreakable nexus between their freedom and this book.
—Patrick Reilly, Nineteen Eighty-Four: *Past, Present, and Future* (Boston: Twayne, 1989), pp. 127–29

MICHAEL SHELDEN ON AUTOBIOGRAPHICAL ELEMENTS IN *NINETEEN EIGHTY-FOUR*

[Michael Shelden (b. 1951) is the author of biographies of Graham Greene (1994) and George Orwell (1991), from which the following extract is taken. Here, Shelden points out the many features in *Nineteen Eighty-Four* that seem to derive from incidents in Orwell's own life.]

It is Orwell's most compelling work, and its enormous success over the years is well deserved, but it is also his most misunderstood work. Endless theories have been put forward to explain its vision of the future, but not many critics have been willing to see how firmly rooted it is in Orwell's past. Almost every aspect of Orwell's life is in some way represented in the book. Winston Smith's yearning for the green wilderness of the

"Golden Country" is very much connected to Orwell's long-standing affection for the lost Edwardian world of his childhood in Henley. The objects of that older world have been discarded as "junk" in Big Brother's world, but Winston tries to hold onto a few pieces of this "junk" as a way of maintaining his links with the past. In a similar way Orwell spent a good deal of time in the 1940s, while he was living in London, haunting junk shops with mountains of old, apparently useless, items from another age. Just as Winston finds a beautiful paperweight in an old shop and clings to it as though it were a kind of life preserver, so Orwell praised junk shops in the *Evening Standard,* in 1946—celebrating the joys of "useless" relics from a time long before Hitler and Stalin and atom bombs. He specifically mentioned his delight at discovering "glass paperweights with pictures at the bottom. There are others that have a piece of coral enclosed in the glass." Winston's, of course, has a piece of coral embedded in it, and he examines it intently, surprised that anything so delicate could survive in a brutal age.

Orwell's experiences of bullying at St. Cyprian's cannot be discounted as an influence on *Nineteen Eighty-Four.* He was working on "Such, Such Were the Joys" when he was in the early stages of writing the novel, and there is an overlapping theme in the two works. Both are concerned with the ways in which people can be manipulated to look up to their tormentors as superior beings who should be respected—even loved—rather than as the objects of the hate they have earned. Young Eric Blair was made to feel guilty because he did not love Mrs. Wilkes, and he took comfort in knowing that, in his heart of hearts, he felt only hatred for her. Likewise, Winston must struggle against the temptation to love Big Brother, fighting back the desire to surrender his hatred in the face of overwhelming power. He feels just as helpless against such power as young Eric felt in the face of Mrs. Wilkes's authority.

For models of authoritarian power at work Orwell could look to incidents from his life in the Indian Imperial Police, his experiences in Barcelona when the government was trying to suppress the POUM, and his encounters with the absurdities of wartime censorship—at the BBC as well as in his ordinary work as a journalist. It is not the case, by any means, that these relatively mild forms of tyranny are worthy of any close compari-

son with Big Brother's nightmarish rule, but all these elements helped give Orwell a certain feel for the life he describes in the novel, a life that is ultimately the work of his imagination, but that is based on real experience. When he describes torture in the novel, for example, he is able to draw on his memories of milder forms of torture—both mental and physical—at St. Cyprian's and in Burma. And when he describes the mindless, never-ending warfare, with bombs exploding randomly every day, he had only to recall the sensations he felt during the Blitz and later during the attacks from Hitler's V-1 flying bombs and V-2 rockets. The cold, drab environment—with its scarcities and bad food—is partly a reflection of conditions in Britain during much of the 1940s.
—Michael Shelden, *Orwell: The Authorized Biography* (New York: HarperCollins, 1991), pp. 430–32

W. J. West on *Nineteen Eighty-Four* and Surveillance

[W. J. West is the author of *Truth Betrayed* (1987) and *Opus Dei: Exploding a Myth* (1987) and the editor of Orwell's *The War Broadcasts* (1985) and *The War Commentaries* (1985). In this extract from his book on *Nineteen Eighty-Four* (1992), West notes that the extensive surveillance used in Orwell's novel to control the population is also widely prevalent in contemporary society.]

The most frightening thing in Orwell's totalitarian world is the constant spying, the telescreen that listens to every word, even when you are asleep and watches every movement, or might be watching, all the time. Since the publication of Peter Wright's memoirs we know that it was not only the Stasi that spied on their fellow citizens. There were always people who knew what was going on and that MI5 used surveillance methods of this kind, but there were not many of them. Orwell's parody would have seemed, indeed, a nightmare of a future world to ordinary citizens. Only the few would know what he was driving at and feel the full force of his satire. By the fifties it was widely known that the Russians would take photographs of people in compromising circumstances in order to blackmail them or publicly humiliate them. Again few would have thought the British would stoop to such levels—it was precisely the sort of thing that generations of Englishmen had been taught was not done, although it was an American who, when he learnt that letters were being opened during the First World War, reacted in horror saying 'Gentlemen do not read each other's mail'. In fact Orwell knew that all these things were being done in Britain during the war and continued after it had ended.

The forty years and more that have passed since Orwell wrote his warning have seen a great levelling in the standards of living in Britain, at least as far as one-time luxuries such as cars, televisions and other consumer durables go, and it is difficult to recall the world Orwell knew. Winston Smith is a member of the party, an elite of a few hundred thousand at most. The inner party would consist of a few tens of thousands. The surveillance and terror that operates in *Nineteen Eighty-Four* was meant for that small number only. The bulk of the population are ignored. The situation in East Germany and Russia was far worse. There it was not just the party members who were spied upon but everyman, unlike *Nineteen Eighty-Four* when being in the party even offered some protection. Mass surveillance in Britain is now possible almost at this level, without any great improvement in technology. Electronic telephone exchanges mean that any phone can be tapped at will without the need for elaborate mechanical operations to fit the taps. The advent of the 'smart card' could soon lead to the 'smart' identity card which would have on it all that the authorities need to know about a person. Medical practices in the south west of England have used such cards for some years and a patient produces a card which is wiped through a viewer to produce, on screen, their case history. If smart identity cards became compulsory, as some government officials have urgently suggested, then anyone stopped would immediately have to produce a card which could be wiped by an officer in his car to reveal all he wanted to know. The stage beyond that, already in use for dogs, is to inject a chip beneath the skin. At the moment the authorities in Britain are only considering this for prisoners and other offenders. This is an Orwellian world that Orwell indeed foresaw but applying to the entire population, not just an elite.

The key phrase always used to justify such ideas is 'The innocent need have nothing to fear'. Whenever that phrase is used in final justification, as it was used in Nazi Germany, communist Russia and no doubt every other totalitarian state since the dawn of history, then infringement of civil liberties is certain and freedom, as it is understood in America, and as it was understood in Britain in the nineteenth century, right through to the days of Sir Wilfrid Lawson, will have passed. The gloss of the consumerist society will not be able to hide what has happened. And the word used to describe this tendency is still 'Orwellian' or, more simply, 'Big Brother'. The justification of the need for such a regime was always, in the past, the fear of communism or invasion, or revolution. With the ending of the cold war and the collapse of the Soviet regime these reasons fall away. What is left is the most human motive of all, the motive of the righteous who have persecuted through the ages: power. As Orwell has O'Brien say when forcing Winston to admit that most absurd untruth, that two and two make five, 'We are the priests of Power'.

—W. J. West, *The Larger Evils:* Nineteen Eighty-Four, *The Truth Behind the Satire* (Edinburgh: Canongate Press, 1992), pp. 190–92

Books by George Orwell

Down and Out in Paris and London. 1933.

Burmese Days. 1934.

A Clergyman's Daughter. 1935.

Keep the Aspidistra Flying. 1936.

The Road to Wigan Pier. 1937.

Homage to Catalonia. 1938.

Coming Up for Air. 1939.

Inside the Whale and Other Essays. 1940.

The Lion and the Unicorn: Socialism and the English Genius. 1941.

Talking to India. (editor) 1943.

Animal Farm: A Fairy Story. 1945.

Critical Essays ⟨Dickens, Dali and Others⟩. 1946.

James Burnham and the Managerial Revolution. 1946.

The English People. 1947.

Politics and the English Language. 1947.

British Pamphleteers I: From the Sixteenth Century to the French Revolution (editor; with Reginald Reynolds). 1948.

Nineteen Eighty-Four. 1949.

Shooting an Elephant and Other Essays. 1950.

England, Your England and Other Essays. 1953.

Collected Essays. 1961.

Collected Essays, Journalism and Letters. Ed. Sonia Orwell and Ian Angus. 1968. 4 vols.

Ten Animal Farm *Letters to His Agent, Leonard Moore.* Ed. Michael Shelden. 1984.

Nineteen Eighty-four: The Facsimile of the Extant Manuscript. Ed. Peter Davison. 1985.

The War Broadcasts. Ed. W. J. West. 1985.

The War Commentaries. Ed. W. J. West. 1985.

Works about George Orwell and Nineteen Eighty-Four

Alldritt, Keith. *The Making of George Orwell.* London: Edward Arnold, 1969.

Allen, Francis A. "*Nineteen Eighty-Four* and the Eclipse of the Private Worlds." *Michigan Quarterly Review* 12 (1983): 517–40.

Atkins, John. *George Orwell: A Literary Study.* 2nd ed. London: Calder & Boyars, 1971.

Beadle, Gordon. "George Orwell and the Death of God." *Colorado Quarterly* 23 (1974): 51–63.

Brander, Lawrence. *George Orwell.* London: Longmans, 1954.

Buitenhuis, Peter, ed. *George Orwell: A Reassessment.* New York: St. Martin's Press, 1988.

Burgess, Anthony. *1985.* London: Arrow Books, 1980.

Calder, Jenni. *Chronicles of Conscience: A Study of George Orwell and Arthur Koestler.* London: Secker & Warburg, 1968.

Carter, Michael. *George Orwell and the Problem of Authentic Existence.* Totowa, NJ: Barnes & Noble, 1985.

Chilton, Paul, and Crispin Aubrey. Nineteen Eighty-Four *in 1984.* London: Comedia Publishing Group, 1983.

College Literature 11, No. 1 (1984). Special *Nineteen Eighty-Four* issue.

Connors, James. " 'Do It to Julia': Thoughts on Orwell's *1984.*" *Modern Fiction Studies* 16 (1970–71): 463–73.

Crick, Bernard. *George Orwell: A Life.* London: Secker & Warburg, 1980.

Edrich, Emanuel. "George Orwell and the Satire in Horror." *Texas Studies in Literature and Language* 4 (1962): 96–108.

Forster, E. M. "George Orwell." In Forster's *Two Cheers for Democracy*. New York: Harvest, 1951, pp. 60–63.

Fyvel, T. R. *George Orwell: A Personal Memoir*. London: Macmillan, 1982.

Greenblatt, Stephen Jay. "George Orwell." In Greenblatt's *Three Modern Satirists: Waugh, Orwell and Huxley*. New Haven: Yale University Press, 1965.

Gross, Miriam, ed. *The World of George Orwell*. New York: Simon & Schuster, 1972.

Hollis, Christopher. *A Study of George Orwell: The Man and His Works*. London: Hollis & Carter, 1956.

Howe, Irving, ed. *1984 Revisited: Totalitarianism in Our Century*. New York: Harper & Row, 1982.

Jensen, Ejner J., ed. *The Future of Nineteen Eighty-Four*. Ann Arbor: University of Michigan Press, 1984.

Kubal, David. *Outside the Whale: George Orwell's Art and Politics*. Notre Dame, IN: Notre Dame University Press, 1972.

Lee, Robert A. *Orwell's Fiction*. Notre Dame, IN: University of Notre Dame Press, 1968.

Leif, Ruth Ann. *Homage to Oceania: The Prophetic Vision of George Orwell*. Columbus: Ohio State University Press, 1969.

Lewis, Wyndham. "Orwell, or Two and Two Make Four." In Lewis's *The Writer and the Absolute*. London: Methuen, 1952, pp. 153–94.

Meyers, Jeffrey. *A Reader's Guide to George Orwell*. London: Thames & Hudson, 1975.

Meyers, Valerie. *George Orwell*. New York: St. Martin's Press, 1991.

Mezciems, Jenny. "Swift and Orwell: Utopia as Nightmare." In *Between Dream and Nature: Essays on Utopia and Dystopia*, ed. Dominic Baker-Smith and C. C. Barfoot. Amsterdam: Rodopi, 1987, pp. 91–112.

Modern Fiction Studies 21, No. 1 (Spring 1975). Special George Orwell issue.

Oxley, B. T. *George Orwell.* 2nd ed. London: Evans Brothers, 1970.

Ranald, Ralph A. "George Orwell and the Mad World: The Anti-Universe of *1984.*" *South Atlantic Quarterly* 66 (1967): 544–53.

Rankin, David. "Orwell's Intention in *1984.*" *English Language Notes* 12 (1975): 188–92.

Rees, Richard. *George Orwell: Fugitive from the Camp of Victory.* London: Secker & Warburg, 1961.

Reilly, Patrick. *George Orwell: The Age's Adversary.* London: Macmillan; New York: St. Martin's Press, 1986.

Roazen, Paul. "Orwell, Freud, and *1984.*" *Virginia Quarterly Review* 54 (1978): 675–95.

Russell, Betrand. "Symptoms of Orwell's *1984.*" In Russell's *Portraits from Memory and Other Essays.* London: George Allen & Unwin, 1956, pp. 221–28.

Sandison, Alan. *The Last Man in Europe: An Essay on George Orwell.* London: Macmillan, 1974.

Slater, Ian. *Orwell: The Road to Airstrip One.* New York: Norton, 1985.

Small, Christopher. *The Road to Miniluv: George Orwell, the State and God.* London: Gollancz, 1975.

Smyer, Richard I. *Primal Dream and Primal Curse: Orwell's Development as a Psychological Novelist.* Columbia: University of Missouri Press, 1979.

Stanksy, Peter, ed. *On* Nineteen Eighty-Four. San Francisco: W. H. Freeman, 1983.

Stansky, Peter, and Abrahams, William. *Orwell: The Transformation.* New York: Alfred A. Knopf, 1980.

———. *The Unknown Orwell.* New York: Alfred A. Knopf, 1972.

Thomas, Edward. *Orwell.* Edinburgh: Oliver & Boyd, 1965.

Todorov, Tzvetan. "Politics, Morality, and the Writer's Life: Notes on George Orwell." *Stanford French Review* 16 (1992): 136–42.

Trilling, Lionel. "George Orwell and the Politics of Truth." In Trilling's *The Opposing Self.* New York: Viking Press, 1959, pp. 151–72.

Voorhees, Richard. *The Paradox of George Orwell.* West Lafayette, IN: Purdue University Studies, 1961.

Watson, George. "Orwell's Nazi Renegade." *Sewanee Review* 94 (1986): 486–95.

Williams, Raymond. *Orwell.* London: Fontana, 1984.

Winnifrith, Tom, and William V. Whitehead. *1984 and All's Well?* London: Macmillan, 1984.

Wykes, David. *A Preface to Orwell.* London: Longman, 1987.

Young, John Wesley. *Totalitarian Language: Orwell's Newspeak and Its Nazi and Communist Antecedents.* Charlottesville: University Press of Virginia, 1991.

Zwerdling, Alex. *Orwell and the Left.* New Haven: Yale University Press, 1974.

Index of Themes and Ideas

AMPLEFORTH, and his role in the novel, 19

ANIMAL FARM, and how it compares, 27, 38

BIG BROTHER: as Antichrist, 33–34; and his role in the novel, 5, 9, 12, 23, 24, 26, 41; and television, 60

BRAVE NEW WORLD (Huxley), and how it compares, 32–33

BROTHERHOOD, THE, and its role in the novel, 10, 17, 22

BURNHAM, JAMES, Orwell influenced by, 44–46

CHARRINGTON, MR., and his role in the novel, 14, 15, 19, 26

CHESS GAME, as symbol, 55–56

CHRISTMAS CAROL, A (Dickens), and how it compares, 64

COMING UP FOR AIR, and how it compares, 39

DOUBLETHINK, and its role in the novel, 5, 11–12, 13, 18, 28–29

EASTASIA, and its role in the novel, 11, 17–18, 20

EURASIA, and its role in the novel, 11, 17–18

FAMILY LIFE, as theme, 39–40, 58

GLASS PAPERWEIGHT, as symbol, 14, 62, 66

GOLDEN COUNTRY, as symbol, 11, 15, 56, 66

GOLDSTEIN, EMMANUEL: book by, 18, 29, 45; and his role in the novel, 10, 17, 20, 26, 28, 41, 58

INGSOC, and its role in the novel, 18, 30, 41

INNER PARTY, and its role in the novel, 10, 12, 17, 19, 25, 48, 69

JULIA: as member of the Junior Anti-Sex League, 10, 15, 25; rebellion of, 15, 25; and her role in the novel, 5, 11, 12; Smith's betrayal of, 22–23, 25, 29, 56; Smith's relationship with, 14–19, 25–26, 57, 59

JUNIOR ANTI-SEX LEAGUE, and its role in the novel, 10, 15, 25, 39, 43, 51

KEEP THE ASPIDISTRA FLYING, and how it compares, 37, 39

LANGUAGE, as theme, 12, 16, 46–49, 52–54

MINISTRY OF LOVE, and its role in the novel, 9, 19–24

MINISTRY OF TRUTH: past history "rectified" by, 12, 13–14, 18, 61–63; and its role in the novel, 9, 10

MORAL CHOICE, as theme, 63–65

NEWSPEAK: dictionary of, 12, 16, 26; and its role in the novel, 5, 41, 42, 52–53

NINETEEN EIGHTY-FOUR: attacked as betrayal of leftist cause, 29–30, 47; autobiographical elements of, 65–67; as comical, 29; composition of, 8; and contemporary surveillance, 67–69; as culmination of Orwell's career, 36–38; ending of, 23–24, 54–56, 59–60, 63–65; environmental aspects of, 49–52; evil in, 33–34; Huxley on, 32–33; as inept narrative, 5–6; Orwell on, 29–30; as prophecy, 5–6, 34–36, 41–42, 47; realism of, 28–29; scope of, 30–32; sensationalism of, 29, 57; and television, 59–60; terrifying quality of, 27, 31; virtues and flaws of, 28–29; women in, 57–59

O'BRIEN: as intellectual figure, 38; as member of the Inner Party, 10, 25, 69; sadism of, 5; Smith's dream of, 11, 17; as Smith's interrogator, 20–24, 25, 43–46, 48, 55–56; Smith's rendezvous with, 16, 17, 25, 48; Smith's "romance" with, 57

OCEANIA: Hate Week in, 12, 17; and post–World War II population explosion, 49–52; and its role in the novel, 9–25; static quality of life in, 35–36; at war, 11, 17–19, 50

ORWELL, GEORGE: anger of, 37–38; in the Burmese Imperial Police, 7, 66; death of, 8; as "democratic socialist," 53; intellectuals distrusted by, 37–38; international recognition achieved by, 53; life of, 7–8; linguistic influence of, 52–54

OUTER PARTY, and its role in the novel, 9

PARSONS, and his role in the novel, 12, 19, 26

PARTY, THE: capitalist corporations compared to, 41–42; motivations of, 18, 22, 38, 44–46, 50, 69; personal love destroyed by, 16–17, 25, 39–40, 42–44, 51; and its role in the novel, 9–25; slogans of, 10, 22–23, 42; telescreens employed by, 9, 11, 12, 13, 14, 19, 42, 55, 67; women in, 58

"POLITICS AND THE ENGLISH LANGUAGE," and how it compares, 52–53, 54

POWER, as theme, 18, 22, 28, 38, 44–46, 69

PROLES, and their role in the novel, 13, 14, 17, 19, 29, 38, 58

ROOM 101, and its role in the novel, 19–22, 23, 29

SELFHOOD, as theme, 46–49

SEXUALITY, as theme, 10, 13, 15–16, 25, 31, 34, 39–40, 42–44, 51–52

SMITH, WINSTON: arrest of, 19; confession of, 20; as a consumer, 60; diary of, 10–11, 13, 14, 21, 47–49, 61–63; dreams of, 11, 16, 17, 19, 47; as the last man, 22, 47; rats feared by, 16, 23, 29; reader's response to, 49; "reintegration" of, 19–24, 25, 35, 43–46, 55–56, 59–60; and his role in the novel, 9–25; sanity of, 19, 21; search for the past by, 9, 11, 13–14, 16, 20–21, 25, 29, 55–56, 61–63; thoughtcrime committed by, 10–11; as weak character, 5–6, 48–49

SOVIET UNION, as a subject of the novel, 27, 28–29, 41, 45, 47

SUCH, SUCH WERE THE JOYS, and how it compares, 39, 66

SWIFT, JONATHAN, Orwell compared to, 6, 27, 45

SYME, and his role in the novel, 12, 16, 26

THOUGHT POLICE, and their role in the novel, 9, 12, 13, 19, 23, 26

TOTALITARIANISM, as theme, 27, 29–30, 31, 34–36, 40–42, 47

TWO MINUTES HATE: and displaced eroticism, 43; and its role in the novel, 5, 10

UNCLE TOM'S CABIN (Stowe), and how it compares, 5

WE (Zamiatin), and how it compares, 42–44

WELLS, H. G., Orwell compared to, 5